Create Your Best Life:

Unleash Your Charisma and Confidence to
Change the World

Tom Marcoux

America's Communication Coach
and author of *Be Heard and Be Trusted*

A QuickBreakthrough Publishing Edition

Copyright © 2013 Tom Marcoux Media, LLC
ISBN: 0615835821
ISBN-13: 978-0615835822

All rights reserved. No part of this book may be reproduced or transmitted in any form by any means electronic or mechanical, including photocopying, recording or by any information storage and retrieval system without written permission from the publisher.

QuickBreakthrough Publishing is an imprint of Tom Marcoux Media, LLC. More copies are available from the publisher, Tom Marcoux Media, LLC. Please call (415) 572-6609 or write TomSuperCoach@gmail.com

or visit www.TomSuperCoach.com

or Tom's blog: www.BeHeardandBeTrusted.com

This book was developed and written with care. Names and details were modified to respect privacy.

Disclaimer: The author and publisher acknowledge that each person's situation is unique, and that readers have full responsibility to seek consultations with health, financial, spiritual and legal professionals. The author and publisher make no representations or warranties of any kind, and the author and publisher shall not be liable for any special, consequential or exemplary damages resulting, in whole or in part, from the reader's use of, or reliance upon, this material.:

Other Books by Tom Marcoux:
- Be Heard and Be Trusted: How to Get What You Want
- Nothing Can Stop You This Year!
- Darkest Secrets of Persuasion and Seduction Masters
- Darkest Secrets of Charisma
- Darkest Secrets of Negotiation Masters
- Darkest Secrets of the Film and Television Industry Every Actor Should Know
- Darkest Secrets of Making a Pitch to the Film and Television Industry
- Darkest Secrets of Film Directing
- Darkest Secrets of Small Business Marketing

Praise for *Create Your Best Life - Change the World:*
"This is an uplifting and practical book. You'll learn skills in persuasion, charisma, confidence, influence and emotional strength—all vital elements to help you positively change the world. To make a dream come true, you'll need to get people enrolled in your vision. This is *the book* that helps you get great things done!" – Dr. JoAnn Dahlkoetter, author of *Your Performing Edge* and coach to CEOs and Olympic Gold Medalists

"When you want to get big things done, persuasion skills are crucial. Tom Marcoux shows you how to develop new reflexes and responses so you can become even more influential under stressful situations. As a journalist and publicist, I've observed how some people come across as charismatic and influential, while others fail to get their message across. Tom Marcoux reveals methods that anyone can use to enhance their charisma and influence—and make a big, positive difference in this world."
– Danek S. Kaus, author of the best-selling *You Can Be Famous: Insider Secrets to Getting Free Publicity* and founder of freepublicityforyou.com

"I like author and executive coach Tom Marcoux's distinction between Hard-Headed Convincing and his **effective** Soft-Hearted Persuasion. Marcoux's methods of developing confidence help the reader feel stronger and take effective action." – David Barron, co-author of *Power Persuasion* and founder of newhampshirehypnosis.com

Praise for Tom Marcoux's Other Work
"In *Darkest Secrets of Persuasion and Seduction Masters*, learn useful countermeasures to protect yourself from being darkly manipulated."
– David Barron, co-author, *Power Persuasion*

"In *Be Heard and Be Trusted*, Tom's advice on how to remain true to yourself and establish authentic rapport with clients is both insightful and reality based. He [shows how] to establish oneself as a credible expert."
-Arthur P. Ciaramicoli, Ed.D., Ph.D., author *The Curse of the Capable*, and *The Power of Empathy*

"*Nothing Can Stop You This Year* is a treasure trove of tips, tools, and terrific ideas—practical, reassuring, and energizing! Tom provides wonderful resources for achieving your goals." – Elayne Savage, Ph.D., author of *Don't Take It Personally! The Art of Dealing with Rejection*

Visit Tom's blog: www.BeHeardandBeTrusted.com

CONTENTS

Dedication and Acknowledgments	i
Book One: Create Your Best Life - Change the World (Persuasion, Charisma, Confidence)	1
Persuasion	11
Charisma	27
Confidence	35
Chapter Two: The P.E.R.S.U.A.D.E. Process of Persuasion	49
Book Two: Influence	85
Book Three: Leverage	93
Book Four: Emotional Strength	109
Book Five: Effective Selling is "Coaching-to-Action"	133
Book Six: Wisdom for Tough Times and Your Power to Excel	163
A Final Word and Springboard to Your Dreams	185
Excerpt from *Be Heard and Be Trusted: How to Use Secrets from the Greatest Communicators to Get What You Want*	188
About the Author Tom Marcoux	198
Special Offer Just for Readers of this Book	200

DEDICATION AND ACKNOWLEDGEMENTS

This book is dedicated to the terrific book and film consultant, and author Johanna E. Mac Leod. It is also dedicated to the other team members. Thanks to Sherry Lusk, David MacDowell Blue, and Danek S. Kaus for editing. Thanks to my father, Al Marcoux, for his concern and efforts for me. Thanks to my mother, Sumiyo Marcoux, a kind, generous soul. Thanks to Judita Bacinskaite for rendering this book's front cover. Thank you Johanna E. Mac Leod for rendering this book's back cover. Thanks to the guest authors Mark Sanborn, Chip Conley, C.J. Hayden, Morgan Rae and Lois Creamer for their articles. Thank you to Higher Power. Thanks to our readers, audiences, clients, my graduate/college students and my team members of Tom Marcoux Media, LLC.

BOOK ONE: CREATE YOUR BEST LIFE - CHANGE THE WORLD (PERSUASION, CHARISMA AND CONFIDENCE)

What would you love to do? Do you feel something is missing in your life—something just out of reach?

You could have more and better times with family and friends—more vacations and joy. Also, more career and financial success as well as genuine fulfillment.

This particular topic means a lot to me. Why? Today, as I write this, one of my college students reels from the news her sister died in a car accident. The sister was only eighteen years old.

When we're touched by death, many considerations shrink and drift away. The most important parts of our lives step into the foreground.

But 18?! I hope the sister had the chance to pack a lot of living in those few years.

I shared the above details because I'm inviting *you* to pack a lot living into one lifetime. Realize the brief amount of time we have to breathe and do anything on this earth, and make the most of every minute of it.

This Book Empowers You in the Areas of Persuasion, Influence, Leverage, and Emotional Strength.

The rest of this book you will hopefully find upbeat, inspiring, and practical in the areas of persuasion, influence, leverage, and emotional strength. These four elements help you get massive cooperation so that you can live on a high level of personal enjoyment and career success.

Let's talk about you truly enjoying your life.

Listen close. I'm good at coaching people to do extraordinary things:
- gather a team and complete a big project
- produce a first feature film
- write a first novel or non-fiction book
- perform well in a job interview and gain a job
- gain an internship at Donna Karan International
- win the Charles Schwab Scholarship
- make speeches that get standing ovations—even when the person was truly shy
- speak and listen with compassion and enhance relationships

Now, it's my honor to be your coach through this book.

You and I now begin an important work.

Your playing small does not serve the world. There is nothing enlightened about shrinking so that other people won't feel insecure around you. We are all meant to shine, as children do. We were born to make manifest the glory of God that is within us. It's not just in some of us; it's in everyone. And as we let our own light shine, we unconsciously give other people permission to do the same. As we are liberated from our own fear, our presence automatically liberates others. – Marianne Williamson

When I talk about create your best life, I'm talking about creating your personal life of joy and fulfillment. Already you have embarked on a sacred work. How? You have made sure there is one less miserable person on this planet—you! That really helps.

That's the first step of changing the world.

When I write about "changing the world," courage is involved because I'm standing up for an idea—something deep in my heart—that others may question.

The first time I wrote the title of this book and attached a subtitle of "change the world," I felt a rush of joy and excitement. I called a close friend and immediately—like a terrible reflex—he said, "Change *your* world." He *diminished* the idea.

I know he was trying to be helpful. Perhaps, he thought that "change the world" might reduce sales. Some cynical people might scoff at the magnitude of "change the world." Fine. I'm *not* writing for them.

I am writing for *you*. Something positive waits to be created by you, to be expressed by you.

Now, I'll coach you through this book so that you'll learn how to create your best life—and change the world.

Whether we're here for 18 or 88 years, our time remains limited.

It's your *choice*.

What do you choose today?

I invite you to choose living your best life. Let's view "best life" as living in ways in which . . .
- you feel fully alive
- you enjoy laughter, wonder, and delightful surprises
- you feel on purpose
- you feel that you make a difference and that your life has meaning

- you enjoy loving and close relationships
- your work has meaning and value that is important to you and to the people you serve through your efforts.

Changing the World Is About Ripples Outward

Realize we do change the world. We know that a kind word can brighten someone's whole afternoon. We do not know how far the positive ripples extend throughout the world, but they do go beyond our immediate circle.

So, do you want to change the world? Then, unleash your charisma and confidence.

Realize that "The Numbers" Do *Not* Negate A Positive Step

Too often, people get caught up in diminishing what they're doing by referring to supposedly small numbers. They say things like "There were only ten people in the room" or "I only sold 3,000 copies of my book." People actually let the fear of small numbers stop them from taking action. That's a real problem.

They need to realize that there is a ripple effect, that supporting one person leads to that person being helpful to another person and so forth.

I realize that numbers like 10 and 3,000 are not anywhere near the 80 million copies sold of *The DaVinci Code*. But I submit to you that influencing 10 human beings—or even one—is still important!

Further, because of the ripple effect, we don't know how far our influence extends. For example, some researchers suggest that people regularly interact with 250 people (perhaps, more now that we're so active with social media). So 10 x 250 equals 2,500. Potentially your interaction with ten people can touch 2,500. I know this to be true. A friend created an image (with a powerful observation) that he shared on Facebook with a few friends which has been seen by 5,017 people.

Another point: It takes just one person to make a big difference for other people. Several years ago, a college instructor addressed 26 students at Reed College on the topic of calligraphy. But one particular person was listening—Steve Jobs. As Jobs related to a Stanford University audience:

"I decided to take a calligraphy class . . .I learned [about] what makes great typography great. It was beautiful, historical, artistically subtle in a way that science can't capture, and I found it fascinating. [Ten] years later, when we were designing the first Macintosh computer, it all came back to me. And we designed it all into the Mac. It was the first computer with beautiful typography. If I had never dropped in on that single course in college, the Mac would have never had multiple typefaces or proportionally spaced fonts. And since Windows just copied the Mac, it's likely that no personal computer would have them."

Now, you can see the above example of the ripple effect.

We can change the world one thought at a time, one child at a time, one family at a time, one community at a time, one city, one state and one country at a time. – Bryant McGill

Do you notice that it begins with "one thought at a time"?

All the darkness in the world cannot extinguish the light of a single candle. – St. Francis of Assisi

You are that single candle. This book helps you expand

your influence. And remember, each kind action means a lot. Did you call someone in the recent week and share a good moment or two with them? You changed their world for a time. Let go of the "numbers." Did you change them for a lifetime? That's not the point. You are part of the bright section of the tapestry of their life.

We do not remember days, we remember moments.
– Cesare Pavese

You do change the world. Every kind act starts a ripple effect; often we witness more kindness.

Again, let go of the "numbers." I know a good writer, but he does *not* finish projects. He chooses to not self-publish any of his work. He worries maybe only 1,000 people will buy his book. I know someone else who frets if she starts a blog only 100 people would read it.

They are missing two vital points. Every person you serve is valuable. Secondly, any serious writer or artist realizes that we learn by doing. Do you want to get better at something? Then complete projects.

What about the woman who frets about getting only 100 readers of a blog she begins? If she sticks with it, perhaps later she'll start a *different* blog, and it will be a hit because the timing and subject just happen to be right. In writing the first blog and series of articles, she hones her craft, giving her the skills needed to succeed in her subsequent projects.

And what about blogs? They are valuable in and of themselves as huge reservoirs of practical information, but they can also be springboards to other successful endeavors. You may recall the blog that resulted in the book *Julie and Julia: 365 Days, 524 Recipes, 1 Tiny Apartment Kitchen* by Julie Powell. The book served as inspiration for the feature film

Julie and Julia starring Meryl Streep (as Julia Child), Amy Adams (as Julie Powell), and Stanley Tucci (as Julia Child's husband). The $40 million film earned over $129 million at the box office. None of that would have happened if Julie Powell had gotten discouraged by her "numbers" and discontinued her blog at Day #8.

When we appeared together as guests on a radio show, author Richard Carlson told me that *Don't Sweat the Small Stuff* (a huge best-seller) was his tenth book. He *honed his craft* through nine other books that had varying levels of readership.

Further, many times a person needs to go through a failure or two to get his or her footing. For example, George Lucas' first feature film, *THX 1138* (1971), was a box office flop, but it ignited a flame in him. Lucas really applied himself and studied with Joseph Campbell, renowned scholar who identified the mono-myth (also known as "the hero's journey" which is a structure of storytelling that appears across the world in various cultures). From Campbell's guidance, Lucas carefully crafted *Star Wars* (1977), which did remarkably well in the marketplace.

For Lucas and other artists, there is a learning curve.

We learn by doing.

This Book Reveals Innovative Methods to Help You Expand Your Influence

Over a decade, I have been guiding clients and graduate students. They've learned to persuade with great ease and skill. I've innovated a process helping people use Soft-Hearted Persuasion and avoiding the negative habits of Hard-headed Convincing. In just a few pages, I will share with you just how Soft-Hearted Persuasion can help you make your dreams come true.

Also, in the next section I will introduce another valuable distinction: my P.I.E. Model. For over 25 years I have studied and trained to help people rise to their best performances. (By the way, it's easy to remember P.I.E. because many of us want a bigger slice of life's pie.)

I've learned that mere mental constructs are *not* enough to achieve transformation. Research data suggests that 93% of people's decision-making occurs on the unconscious level. So my P.I.E. Model includes more than a rational principle; it reaches your subconscious mind and helps you develop new behavior patterns.

The P.I.E. Model:
P - principle
I - inquiry
E - emotional strength

I summarize how important the above three elements are in concert in this way:

Begin with a Principle. Then dig deep, Inquiring and finding your own answers. Finally, proceed on a new course through your improved Emotional Strength.

Creating a best possible life and changing the world both mean facing fear.

This book helps you expand your skills of persuasion and influence. Still you may face situations when you feel uncertain—especially if you seek to change the world.

Fortunately, I've learned that starting with kindness and a good intention actually frees you to express yourself and invite people to collaborate with you.

The more you are motivated by love, the more fearless and free your action will be. – The Dalai Lama

The methods shared in the *Charisma* and *Confidence* sections of this book have helped my clients and graduate students press through fearful thoughts and perform at their best. They will do the same for you. Further, the section on *Emotional Strength* will help you take consistent and effective action.

Imagine living your life on a new level and doing what you *love* to do.

Let's Begin.

PERSUASION

Our conversation about persuasion will include:

a) Make the Shift from Hard-Headed Convincing to Soft-Hearted Persuading
b) Charisma
c) Confidence

Before we go further, let's examine why persuasion is important in the first place. To change the world, you need to enlist cooperation from other people. We succeed in great part related to our ability to get support and appropriate action from other people.

Top successful people I've interviewed have consistently showed a trait: They're persuasive.

Make the Shift from Hard-headed Convincing to Soft-Hearted Persuading

When you want more and better in your life, your emotions become engaged. There is something we really need to notice: When something's really important to us, we start to get pushy. For example, if a loved one's health is involved, we're likely to use language like "You need to—" and "You should—."

Does that really work? How often have you seen friends or family members quickly agree and do what the other person presses upon them?

Let's look at it another way. How do you feel when people start issuing orders and pressing their viewpoints down your throat? Irritated, perhaps upset, I imagine. I call the forceful pressing of a viewpoint upon another person *Hard-headed Convincing*.

One reason I use the words "hard-headed" is that many of us become stubborn and continue in behaviors that do *not* work. We may feel urgency and righteousness and allow this position to "grant us permission" to keep doing what's not working. I call that hard-headed.

Another reason I refer to hard-headed is that we may have a disconnect between what we're saying (from our head) and where empathy resides (in our heart).

Hard-Headed Convincing

When you "convince someone," it's a forceful act. The person sits in their position, and you try to unseat them. In convincing, you "overcome objections" (an old-style selling term). To overcome an objection carries the energy of overwhelming the other person's original position, perhaps through logic or some form of emotional appeal. Several years ago, selling and overcoming objections were about having clever phrases and techniques to "handle objections." But the truth is: No one wants to be handled, overcome, or pushed into submission.

Definitions of *convince* include: "to overcome by argument" and "to bring (as by argument) to belief, consent, or a course of action" (*The Merriam Webster Dictionary*).

Here's another telling detail: When you look at the original Latin, "convince" includes *vincere* which means "to conquer." No wonder many people resent a "convincing" approach. It feels manipulative.

At this point, we can conclude that attempts at convincing feel like being pushed.

However, there's another intense detail: If you think you must "convince" someone, you may procrastinate. Why? Often we dread the whole process. We can imagine the distasteful resistance ahead.

Further, it's hard to let go of habits of trying to convince another. Why? The more intense your emotions, the more likely that you'll fall back into negative habits of Hard-Headed Convincing. I've seen this often with friends and family and even in myself. I've also seen attempts at Hard-headed Convincing in a number of workplaces, too.

There is something better: *Soft-Hearted Persuading.*

Soft-Hearted Persuading
The essence of Soft-Hearted Persuading is eliciting the other person's reasons for action. That's the opposite of Hard-Headed Convincing, which is about ramming your reasons down their throat.

Here's another way to view the differences:

Hard-Headed Convincing vs. Soft-Hearted Persuading
Telling ....vs. Asking and Listening
Ramming Your Reasons
Down Their Throat...............vs. Eliciting *Their* Reasons

When I talk about *persuading*, I'm using the term in a truly specific way. I'm talking about enticing someone to go along with you. A key part of this process is your focus on their well-being. You make sure that they get benefits from cooperating with you. When you persuade someone, you begin with their well-being in mind. You walk over to their position, and then you metaphorically stand together and look at *what is important to the other person*. How? You use the first method below: Ask a gentle question and listen well.

Here are four methods of Soft-Hearted Persuasion:

1) Ask Gentle Questions and Listen Well
A gentle question is one that is easy to answer, and sometimes the other person actually feels good to express herself with her answer.

Soft-Hearted Persuasion Questions:
- "How did it feel when ___?"
- "What's most important to you about ___?"
- "Ideally, what would you like to happen?"

Not only do you need to listen well, you need to show that you have heard the person. Aim to incorporate some of their words as you express what you heard.

You can use this pattern:
- "I heard you to say _____. Do I have that about right?"

The person will either agree or offer you some clarification. In any case, they know that you're placing your attention on them.

2) Tell A Story (give them an experience)
Asking a gentle question and listening well gives you a clue as to which story to tell. You want your story to be

aligned with the person's priorities and values.

The center of persuading is giving the person an experience—telling a story that gives the person an experience of the value that you offer.

How does telling a story persuade someone? It gets under the radar; that is, they do *not* have something to directly resist. Instead, they go through an experience. From childhood, we're all conditioned to pay attention to and enjoy stories.

When telling a story, make things vivid. A mere phrase like "I'm a people person" does not give the person an experience.

Here's an example:

At one point in my career, I interviewed with a new college so that I might serve as an adjunct lecturer. The interviewer asked, "With all your success as an entrepreneur, why do you want to teach here?"

I replied, "Several years ago, I was walking down the hallway of the college I graduated from. I was there for a Grand Reunion. As I walked past the empty classrooms, I suddenly got this intuition, 'I want to teach!' Some people fall into teaching. Maybe they want to do research. But I was *called*. I felt 'I want to teach,' and within six months, I was at DeAnza College speaking to an audience of 203 people. I watch the audience's faces and body language. I can see when they find something I say to be useful to them."

How is this story persuasive? The interviewer experienced how I felt a *calling*. Also, I gave some word pictures about "watching the audience's faces and body language . . . when they find something I say to be useful to them." The implication was that my heart was dedicated to serving people as an educator.

3) The "1 to 10 Method" to Uncover Their Reasons

This "1 to 10 Method" is truly helpful when you want to elicit the other person's possible reasons for changing their behavior.

You use this language initially:

"On a scale of 1-10, 10 being the highest, how ready are you to do _____?"

When they answer, respond with something like "Why wasn't it 3 [or 2]?"

I first learned of the *1 to 10 process* plus "Why wasn't it 3?" from the work of psychologist Dr. Michael Pantalon.

To make this clear, I'll share an example.

Susan turns to her husband, Jack, and says, "Jack, I wonder how important exercising is to you. On a scale of 1 to 10, 10 being the highest, how ready are you to do some form of regular exercise?"

"4," Jack replies.

"Why wasn't it 3?"

"What?"

"You said 4. I'm wondering why you didn't say 3," Susan says.

"Well . . . I feel I need to do something. My father had a heart attack at 52, and I've gained weight, and I'm now his weight when he had the heart attack."

"That sounds like a big concern," Susan says.

"Well, there's you and the kids and I—"

So we can see in the above dialogue that Susan is *not* pressing her reasons upon Jack. Neither is she trying to use logic on him to push him into a corner and agree with her reasoning. Her attempt to encourage Jack to exercise avoids bringing up needless resistance from him.

4) Ask the "What has to happen?" Question

For a job interview, ask the question: "In order for you to know someone is the ideal candidate for this position, what has to happen?"

Why is this phrasing helpful? You do *not* put the person on the spot. You're *not* asking, "What does it take for me to get the position?"

"What has to happen?" opens the door to learning what is most important to the other person.

One of my college students used this question to gain an internship at Donna Karan International, headquartered in New York City. How? In response to my student's question, the interviewer's demeanor changed, and she started informing my student about the next steps in the multiple interview process and how to prepare for such steps.

Now, I'll make a bold statement: Soft-Hearted Persuading Builds Up Your Own Happiness!

Just on the pragmatic level, would you feel better if you knew that your conversation with someone would light them up and brighten their day? Or putting it another way — do you look forward to trying to force someone to make a change?

Just imagine how much better you'd feel if you knew how to positively influence another person.

We're talking about persuading.

Persuading takes more effort. You really need to think through the process and engage your intuition and feelings. You need to imagine how the person may feel. Persuading involves preparing good questions and listening closely. Why is this so important? I sum it up with this phrase: *I can't persuade you if I don't know you.*

My clients and graduate students tend to memorize "I can't persuade you if I don't know you" since it encapsulates *the value of asking good questions and listening well.*

When Their Well-Being Combines With Your Well-Being

I held a conversation with students in one of my public speaking classes. Trudy said, "I'm afraid that when I need the job, I just naturally push for what I want." Sarah continued, "And what do you mean about their [the employer's] well-being? I just want a job!"

As I responded to them, I brought up a couple of points. First, if you know how competent you are and that you're going to work hard at the new job, you're solving a problem for the employer. They need a trustworthy, competent, and dedicated employee.

With a good match of employee and job, at least four people enjoy benefits: you as employee, the employer, their customer, and your co-worker.

The Soft-Hearted Persuasion process reminds us to look for the benefits the other person's wants and to help her voice what she wants.

How to Install Soft-Hearted Persuasion Methods into Your Behaviors
(Using the P.I.E. Model)

In order to make big dreams come true in my own life, I have consistently studied data, earned a degree in psychology, and have observed methods that my clients have used successfully.

I first learned about the power of using *a principle of effective human behavior.* A principle is "a comprehensive and fundamental law . . . a rule or code of conduct" (*The Merriam-Webster Dictionary*). I look upon a *principle* as "an action or plan of action based on something true." For example, there's a phrase: "If in doubt, leave it out." The phrase can indicate that "one is better off to listen only to oneself and drop something because it can cause harm." I know some people who live by the principle of "If in doubt, leave it out."

However, many years ago, I learned that good ideas on their own are *not* enough. I also learned that people do not change until they're good and ready—and not before.

So I've formed my P.I.E. Model (that I mentioned earlier.) We can look on P.I.E. as the process of taking the ideas and installing them in you so that you're more resourceful in a stressful situation.

P.I.E. stands for
Principle
Inquiry
Emotional Strength

As I shared earlier:

Begin with a Principle. Then dig deep, Inquiring and finding your own answers. Finally, proceed on a new course through your improved Emotional Strength.

An important point here is that a good idea is *not* enough. What counts is action and implementation. That's where Inquiry comes in. An old phrase is: "Someone with a big enough why [reason] can endure any how [method]."

The big reason actually supports your emotional strength, and you need such strength to persist in your new behaviors.

This process will become clearer with an example.

My client Jill and her husband Stewart share a home office. Stewart has the habit of writing his notes on scraps of paper and leaving them all around. This creates clutter and related chaos.

Jill's old approach [Hard-Headed Convincing] was to not speak up until she was fed up and upset. She asked me how she might apply Soft-Hearted Persuasion to this situation.

Our conversation went in this manner:

What do you want?

Jill: I want the clutter to go away. I'm damn tired of having to clean up after Stewart.

I hear you. This sounds like the tip of something bigger. For now, let's start with the clutter topic. How would you usually go about attempting to get Stewart to change?

Jill: I'd tell him: "This is driving me nuts! It bothers me to have this clutter in my way."

How would that go?

Jill: He'd just reply with vague ideas about how he needs notes on separate pages because writing on the back of a sheet could get him to miss details. He'd say it's happened before.

Okay. Tell me again about the reason for Stewart to change his behavior with notes and clutter.

Jill: It's driving me nuts. It bothers me.

I hear you. Whose reasons are these?

Jill: These reasons just make sense. . . . Okay . . . They're my reasons.

Good point. So the idea with Soft-Hearted Persuasion is to elicit Stewart's reasons.

From that point, I shared gentle questions that Jill could use.

Questions like:
- "I'm wondering . . . how are things going with your notes on all the separate pieces of paper?"
- "What most important to you about ___?"

But here's the vital part: Jill needs to do her own Inquiry. The reason? So that she has the Emotional Strength to change her own behaviors.

Look at these questions:

- What are my default behaviors? (Do I use Hard-Headed Convincing?)
  - Does that work?
  - What do I really want?
  - What pain is caused by my ineffective default behaviors?
  - How much do I want to be free of that pain?
  - How would my life be better if I applied Soft-Hearted Persuasion?

I realize that the above questions seem like a lot to work with. The point for Inquiry is to get real motivation, that is, real emotional power so that you do the necessary work to implement the new behaviors.

Using *Inquiry*, Jill came up with these answers: "I don't want to be a 'nag.' I want to protect my marriage. I want Stewart to feel loved by me. I want to feel good and loving toward Stewart."

The Result of Inquiry is that you create Emotional Strength to put in energy, work, and persistence to change your own behaviors.

Two Elements of Emotional Strength

First, you need emotional strength for persistent efforts. Second, you build up your emotional strength as you do new empowered behaviors.

Here's a summary of Jill's Experience with the P.I.E. Model:

Problem: Stewart's writing on scraps of paper creates maddening clutter that Jill is stuck with.

Principle: Use Soft-Hearted Persuasion skills to guard her marriage. [An alternative principle is: Stewart will change when he has his own reasons. Jill needs to help him uncover them.]

Inquiry: Jill identifies what really empowers her to change how she communicates with Stewart. "I don't want to be a 'nag.' I want to protect my marriage. I want Stewart to feel loved by me. I want to feel good and loving toward Stewart."

Emotional Strength: Now Jill has the energy to change her behavior. Now she is willing to study and practice Soft-Hearted Persuasion skills. She learned methods with her coach (me). She rehearsed with her best friend Chandra and me.

Important Point: It is the *actual experience* of her own

reasons that makes Jill's Emotional Strength level rise. Her understanding changes so that her emotions become involved in a useful direction.

Another Vital Point: Rehearsal is required to use Soft-Hearted Persuasion skills.

Rehearsal yields something extraordinary: a *New Choice Conditioned Response*. When rehearsing, you condition yourself into a new behavior. You literally build new neural pathways in the brain. The idea is to choose new empowered behaviors and then condition yourself into actually performing them. For Jill, the New Choice Conditioned Response was for her to ask supportive questions to help Stewart find his own reasons for changing his behavior.

A summary of how things went for Jill and Stewart:

Jill observed whether having scraps of paper around caused any trouble for Stewart. She noticed that Stewart became frustrated because he could not find a particular piece of paper. Jill rehearsed with me and her friend Chandra. And she let two days go by before she calmly talked about the clutter situation.

"Stewart, I'm wondering about something. Is this an okay time for you to talk about something?" Jill asked.

"Yeah. This is fine," he replied.

"I'm wondering . . . how are things going with having your notes on all the separate pieces of paper?"

"I know where this is going. You hate clutter," Stewart replied.

"That's one detail And I'm wondering about what you're

going through. How is the separate pieces of paper working for you?" she asked.

"I did have trouble finding my notes on the Kerwin project. Damn! It was so frustrating."

"I'm wondering how ready you are to find some new ways to deal with notes like that. On a scale of 1 to 10, ten is completely ready. Where are you?" Jill asked.

"3," he replied.

"So you're at 3 in terms of changing something about the notes on scraps of paper?"

"Yeah."

"Why aren't you at 2?" Jill asked.

"What? Oh . . . I guess, I don't want you frustrated about the clutter."

"I appreciate that. And what about *you*? What about the situation puts you at a 2?" Jill asked.

"Well . . . actually, I can't stand it when I can't find something," Stewart said.

Stewart was on his way to finding his own reasons to look for solutions. Eventually, he started carrying a journal in his pocket. He used Post-it Notes to mark vital pages. Sometimes, he cut pages from his journal and placed them into file folders. Stewart had to find his own way to create a system that he would use.

Again, I emphasize: in order to use Soft-Hearted Persuasion, rehearsal is important.

Starting to use Soft-Hearted Persuasion is like having easy practice sessions when first learning to drive a car.

Soft-Hearted Persuasion takes significant attention—just like learning to drive a car.

Remember Soft-Hearted Persuasion is about eliciting their reason to change behaviors. You are like a facilitator and a guide.

Points to Remember:

Principle: Soft-Hearted Persuasion is about eliciting their reasons.

Your Action:
Rehearse asking gentle questions and listening well.

CHARISMA

The first detail I'll share about charisma is that there are actually three forms. In my book, *Darkest Secrets of Charisma: Overcome the Lies about Personal Magnetism, Get People to Feel Your Charisma and Influence Others with Your Words*, I began with the idea that many of us usually talk about only one type of charisma. People toss in the names Bill Clinton, Ronald Reagan, Oprah Winfrey, and others. Let's call that form of charisma *"Magnetic Charisma."*

Through this section, we'll not only increase your Magnetic Charisma, but we'll also bring out your own *Natural Charm Charisma*. There's something that comes naturally to you: Natural Charm Charisma. This is great news for introverts, who make up 40% of the population: an introvert can shine with natural charm. I'll show you how.

How is Natural Charm Charisma different from Magnetic Charisma? Natural Charm Charisma is about making the other person feel comfortable in your presence. Some people naturally exude compassion and caring.

Magnetic Charisma is about overwhelming attractiveness. Perhaps you are not blessed with an overwhelming form of attractiveness.

However, you *do* possess Natural Charm Charisma. In this book, I'll show you how to get obstacles out of your way to expressing this form of charisma, such as nervousness, feeling unprepared, and hesitation.

You'll also learn about Warm Trust Charisma. You can do simple behaviors that get people to trust you and feel a warm connection with you. Let's face facts. People hire those they trust. We develop uplifting and influential friendships with people with whom we feel a warm connection.

Here's a quick summary related to three types of Charisma:

Natural Charm Charisma includes things you can naturally do to make people comfortable in your presence. Your goal is to get obstacles out of your way (like nervous hand gestures) and let your natural charm shine through. The image: *Take a cover off a glowing light bulb.*

Warm Trust Charisma includes things you can do so that people feel that you're genuine and trustworthy. It's all about a warm connection. The image: *Your hand extends in friendship.*

Magnetic Charisma (or Force of Nature) is overwhelming attractiveness. The image: *A magnet pulls people in.*

My discussion about charisma stands out from other

books on charisma because it reaches you wherever you are. By this I mean that you can improve upon your situation whether you're already comfortable talking to new people or not.

Charisma does NOT mean
— You must be an extrovert.
— You use words perfectly.
— You copy others who possess charisma.

Instead, you learn to unleash the charisma power that already resides in you. When you take action to radiate charisma, you'll get a bonus: You'll feel confident.

In other words, you act your way to feeling empowered.

To get you started, I'll share a method for each of the three forms of charisma.

Natural Charm Charisma
The word charm does not arise in a lot of conversations, but we do hear something like: "Yes, he's a nice guy." In such a situation, the person radiates a form of charisma that gives the impression of "niceness."

I begin by talking about Natural Charm Charisma because it is something we can all aspire to, even those of us who call ourselves introverts. Some of my clients complain that they're introverts. They emphasize that they're good when talking one-on-one but fall apart when addressing a group.

Natural Charm Charisma Method:

Have a series of one-to-one conversations. First, greet audience members and talk with them before your presentation. Ask them a couple of questions and make a connection. Then, when you give your presentation, talk to the friendly faces in the group. When you speak, give a whole paragraph to one person, and then move on to another friendly face for the next paragraph. In this way, you really do have a series of one-to-one conversations.

This method quiets fear. By focusing on one person, you are doing something that you do naturally and well. The bonus is that the people behind that person will feel like you're personally addressing them, too!

Warm Trust Charisma
To create trust, it helps to get the "distractions" out of the way. One such distraction is the disconnect between what your words are saying and what your hands are doing.

Warm Trust Charisma Method:
Get your hands away from each other. Another way I say this is: "Don't pet the cat." By that, I'm referring to a nervous person's habit of stroking one hand with the other in a process known as self-soothing. It's as if you're petting your own hand.

Why is it important to avoid nervous gestures with your hands? If the audience sees your hands fluttering about or picking at nails or drumming away at the podium, they naturally think: "What is this person trying to hide? He looks nervous, as if he's scared of getting caught! Caught at what? What is he up to?"

Such thoughts are often on the subconscious level. In fact,

their emotional brain has been stimulated. The emotional brain is made of the brain stem and amygdala. This part of the brain focuses on one thing: preventing loss. When you look nervous, your listener's emotional brain and subconscious mind conclude: "What does he have to hide? If he's hiding something, I might get hurt here."

So your answer is to avoid stimulating the emotional brain's defenses in your audience. How? Look calm by keeping your hands away from each other.

As I mentioned earlier, Warm Trust Charisma includes things you can do so that people feel that you're genuine and trustworthy. It's a process of creating a warm connection. And to create that feeling of trust, you need to move your body in a way that is congruent with your words. For example, if you say, "I'm confident that my product can save you $5000," but you're wringing your hands, there is a disconnect between your words and your behavior. So the solution again is to keep those hands away from each other.

Standing tall while using wide-open hand gestures makes you look comfortable and strong, regardless of whether you're feeling somewhat nervous on the inside.

Magnetic Charisma (Force of Nature Charisma):
Some people come across as a force of nature. They walk into a room, and it looks like they own the place. Still, realize that magnetic people may *not* feel as confident as they look. There are subtle things that magnetic people do.

Magnetic Charisma Method:

Pause, breathe, and smile. Someone told me once what they noticed when I speak before a group of 600 or more people. They said that I always pause, take a deep breath in, and smile. What does this behavior communicate? Confidence. I know that I'm going to provide valuable information. I know that the audience will have a good time with me. How do I know this? I've rehearsed the speech, gained coaching from my advisors, and studied my craft of public speaking for years.

You don't need to wait for years of experience, though. You can start practicing the pause, breathe, and smile method today.

Why is this technique important? When you smile, you look confident. And the audience responds to you as if you're confident. The positive first impression creates a positive feedback loop. You look confident—>the audience treats you as a confident person—>you feel more confident.

It is easier to act yourself into a better way of feeling than to feel yourself into a better way of action. — O.H. Mowrer

Now that I know about the effectiveness of the pause, breathe, and smile method, I use it on purpose. Even after decades of public speaking, I have times when I feel nervous. In those moments, I decide to pause, breathe, and smile. It calms me down. My deliberate action changes how I feel.

The smile part helps with radiating Magnetic Charisma. Confident people have a natural smile that is welcoming, and it looks like they're really confident! On the other hand, ordinary people may arrive in a room, look around, and frown as their nerves come through. Don't let this happen to you. Practice the pause, breathe, and smile method. When you walk into a room and pause, breathe, and smile, it looks like you own the room. You look comfortable.

Remember, you do *not* need to feel comfortable in order for an audience to perceive you as comfortable and strong. Practice the above methods, perhaps with a trusted friend or family member.

Practice and rehearsal really count. You might also consider joining Toastmasters, a non-profit organization that provides opportunities to practice public speaking before a supportive group.

To change the world, it truly helps to radiate the form of charisma that naturally comes to us. Remember: Natural Charm Charisma, Warm Trust Charisma and Magnetic Charisma.

Points to Remember:
P.I.E. for Charisma

Principle: Use what comes naturally to you. Place your efforts into the form of charisma that resonates with you: Natural Charm Charisma, Warm Trust Charisma or Magnetic Charisma.

Inquiry: What comes naturally to you? Are you a good listener? Then ask the audience a few questions (for example). Have friends told you that you're good at something? Is there a way to incorporate that in how you communicate with people? What's really important to you so that you will devote energy to rehearsal?

Emotional Strength:
(The essence of transformation is consistent rehearsal and creating your New Choice Conditioned Response*.)

Identify which methods you will rehearse. Have multiple people as supporters. (Perhaps, you'll rehearse the opening of a speech with one friend and the ending of the speech with another.)

Consider rehearsing the below methods:

Natural Charm Charisma Method:

Have a series of one-to-one conversations. First, greet audience members and talk with them before your presentation. Ask them a couple of questions and make a connection.

Warm Trust Charisma Method:

Standing tall while using wide-open hand gestures makes you look comfortable and strong, regardless of whether you're feeling somewhat nervous on the inside.

Magnetic Charisma Method:
Pause, breathe, and smile.

---

* New Choice Conditioned Response: When rehearsing you condition yourself into a new behavior. You literally build new neural pathways in the brain. The idea is to choose new empowered behaviors and then condition yourself into actually performing them.

CONFIDENCE

"I won't try that until I feel comfortable about it," and other versions of this statement pop up in our daily lives.

Another limiting statement is "That won't work for me; I don't feel confident about doing that."

When these kinds of statements run a person's life, he or she may be paralyzed into a disempowering life. A life of routine. Perhaps, with fewer lows, but unfortunately with *the absence of true joy and exhilaration.*

But this is **not** for you.

I've studied and trained in methods to improve confidence. Why? Since I was a nine-year-old, I've wanted big, positive things. And I discovered that I'd have to do extraordinary things to make my dreams come true. I'm *not* talking from theory. This is real world experience here!

I've learned that two elements arise related to confidence:

a) experiencing "true confidence" that inspires valuable action

b) feeling confident.

Related to experiencing true confidence, you need to shift

from "I need to feel comfortable" to "I only need to feel capable enough." Successful people I have interviewed demonstrated a particular trait: they did NOT wait to feel comfortable before taking action.

In my book *10 Seconds to Wealth: Master the Moment Using Your Divine Gifts*, I revealed the W.A.K.E. process of true confidence. I'll provide a brief summary and a few significant details to begin this discussion.

Want it from your True Self

To feel confident, you need energy. But if your goal is not your own, then you may find that you just don't feel like making the effort. Your True Self is the source of real personal energy. Your True Self is that part of you that is naturally brilliant and courageous. Many authors and spiritual teachers suggest that your True Self is connected to Higher Power or the goodness of the universe. How exciting and empowering! I've experienced that in my own life. I wanted so much to make films that I stepped away from feeling shy to push myself out in front of people to lead them in making my films. I remember my high school days leading 17 of my fellow students in a fight scene while I made a film called *True Hero*. Some of the kids were bigger than me, and others had greater standing at the school, but my desire to create a film filled me with energy and courage.

Now I ask you: What do you want? What is something from deep in your heart? To experience true confidence, one born of strong personal energy, you need to start with a desire that is stronger than fear.

Courage is not the absence of fear, but rather the judgment that something else is more important than fear. – Ambrose Redmoon

Your desire from your True Self is more important than fear.

Adapt

If you know that you can roll with whatever comes along, that's a great source of confidence and emotional strength. To be reading these words, you have likely adapted to plenty of things so far in life. Now, take those experiences and fortify your feelings of being capable.

In interviewing successful people, I've seen a big difference. Many of them keep their accomplishments (especially those that involved adapting) front and center in their mind. They remind themselves that they are capable and have the capacity to adapt to whatever new things arise.

Keep on learning

No matter what we know or have experienced, a new situation brings new opportunities and new problems. We can use this principle: *When you're learning, you're winning.* In over twenty years of doing projects (feature films, songs, feature film music soundtracks, audio programs, and books), I have learned with each project. Sometimes when I look back, I wish I had known more while doing a particular project. But then I remember: We learn by doing. If you're okay with learning and training before you begin a new project, and you're prepared to learn while you're doing the project, you will have a foundation of solid confidence.

Encourage help

A person once told me, "Going it alone is for suckers." The better news is that you do *not* have to! When you're going to begin something new to you, gather your supporters. For example, I invite my graduate students who enroll in my public speaking class to gather a circle of friends. I suggest: "When you need to rehearse, you can rehearse the two-minute opening of a speech with one friend, the middle of the speech with another friend, and the ending with a third friend. You can even rehearse by calling a friend on your cell phone." I also invite the students to sign up for the Speaking Lab so that they can get more support, some coaching, and rehearsal time.

When you're gathering supporters, remember these two distinctions:

a) Help them first.
b) Make it easy and fun for them to help you.

Some students balk at the idea of "Help them first." They ask, "How can I help someone?" I suggest, "You can contact them and ask, "How are things going?" And then you can listen to them. Listening is friendly and kind—and it's a supportive thing." Avoid merely calling upon people to ask them to do something for you. Be proactive. Call them just to connect and hear them out. They'll appreciate it. And some will even want to help you.

Finally, invest in yourself by hiring a coach or subject expert when you need help. For example, I've hired editors frequently; that's how I've written 19 previous books. Also, I hired two media coaches when I was preparing to launch a new product and to appear on radio and television. It's great to have multiple people watching my back.

"Feeling Comfortable" Is <u>Not</u> the Central Element of Confidence

Let's look at the above W.A.K.E. distinctions closely. You'll likely notice that "feeling comfortable" is *not* the central element. Instead, we're focused on preparing to adapt and getting support.

To act with confidence is to move forward despite fear. Your confidence does *not* arise from your knowing what is going to happen. Your confidence resides in your ability to adapt and learn all through the process. Over the years, I have faced fear many times—particularly when I have done something for the first time: giving my first speech to 697 people, directing my first feature film, recording my first audio program, writing my first book, and teaching my first college class. I was prepared for the fact that I would make mistakes, and I did make some. What helped was getting supporters, mentors, coaches, and editors.

Courage is easier when you're prepared – Tom Marcoux

I prepared as best as I could. For example, I personally drew 805 storyboards for my first feature film. I knew the film backwards and forwards before I stepped onto the movie set.

Courage is the ability to act in the face of fear. – Phil Stutz

Commitment requires an endless series of small painful actions. – Phil Stutz and Barry Michels

Commit to preparation, and you can step forward with true confidence.

And still, people want to feel better as they take courageous action. Hence, we'll now cover *Methods to "Feel Confident."*

Methods to "Feel Confident"

C - calm down through Heart Breathing
O - open your focus to "How are you doing?"
N - note "What would a confident person do?"
F - find things to be impressed about in the person
I - intensify an action
D - deep breathe before you speak
E - energize a good-pattern before under stress
N - notice and improve your posture
T - target "If you're afraid, rehearse"

1. Calm down through Heart Breathing

Place your hand over your heart. Breathe in through your nose. Hold the breath for a moment. Breathe out through your mouth. Some of my clients breathe in and say to themselves, "God relaxes me." Others focus on "I am relaxed." Choose what works for you. I invite you to practice this process every day—even for just 30 seconds. Soon you can just imagine doing this and immediately feel relaxed. For example, sometimes I recline on a seat on a train, and I can immediately relax.

2. Open your focus to "How are *you* doing?"

When I was a shy nine-year-old playing the piano for seniors at a retirement home, I was terrified. My whole focus was on "How am I doing?" and "Am I making a mistake?"

Then, over years of giving speeches, I learned the power of switching to "How are YOU doing?"

The secret is to engage in the moment. Be right there with the person. This is also known as "being present." How do you do this? Watch the other person's face and body language. See how the person is responding and how you can be of service to him or her. When I give a speech, I watch faces and body language, and I modify my words to connect with my audience. Often, I'll ask a gentle question. By "gentle question," I mean a question that is easy for the person to answer and often is enjoyable for the person to answer.

In addition, I often introduce a topic with a question instead of a flat statement. Why? A statement invites resistance. Look at these two details:

a) Women live longer than men.

b) Why do women live longer than men?

Do you see how the question is intriguing?

Another Way to Get to "How are YOU Doing?"

At the beginning of a speech, I often ask: "When you first heard about my topic for today, what were you expecting and hoping that I would talk about?" Soon I'll ask, "What topic would really help you if I address it? I'll write down your questions and topics here [on a whiteboard]."

Do you see how I'm purposely engaging the audience and listening to them? I go on to say, "I'll address these questions as we go along. I do not do a canned speech. This is a real-time event." Often, a get a couple of chuckles with that statement.

I approach a speech with confidence because I'm *not* trying to impress people; my goal is to work with them and serve them.

3. Note "What would a confident person do?"

Ask yourself, "How would a confident person walk?" Also imagine how a confident person would stand. One of my clients pictured Sean Connery as James Bond, and my client would then walk with confidence and poise.

Here's another technique to use when meeting people at a networking event. Let's say three people are standing together talking. Hold a glass of water in one hand and smoothly walk up to them. Listen to the person talking. Take a drink of water, nod and smile at the people. When the speaker pauses, and the others turn toward you, ask a relevant question related to what the person was saying. Or you can simply say, "Hello, I'm [your name], and you are?" Most often, you'll be addressing the speaker, unless one of the listeners addresses you first.

Special Note: I suggest a glass of water because if someone jostles you, water is less troublesome than wine staining someone's clothes. Secondly, at a networking event, you want to be on your toes, and drinking alcohol may dull your senses a bit.

4. Find things to be impressed about in the person

Many people get nervous as they try to impress someone. That's a lot of work. Instead, change your focus and find things to be impressed about in the person you're talking with. Listen to what they emphasize. Find a sincere compliment to express. Here are examples:

- "Wow, you really held your cool in that situation."
- "That's a creative solution. I bet that was well received."
- "I appreciate how you led the group to a more helpful idea."

5. Intensify an action

My training as an actor gave me the paradigm of focusing on simple actions. For example, for some scenes, I could cry on cue simply by touching my heart.

To "intensify an action" is about focusing. Let's face it.

Many of us at any given moment are scattered. Think of all the multi-tasking going on. Even as I write this I'm listening to music.

So how does one focus? Pick an objective. *Objective* is a word used often by actors. When the actor is clear on the character's objective (what he or she wants), the actor is focused. The actor's performance will radiate truth.

Further, to intensify an action, tie a simple action to your objective. What can the simple action be? *Listening well*, for example.

Here are some examples of combining an action with an objective [objective in italics]:
- I'll listen well, and *he'll feel good* when talking with me.
- I'll smile, and *she'll feel welcome* at this networking event.

You can see the simple actions of listening and smiling culminating in a positive result for both you and your contact.

6. Deep breathe before you speak

My assistant said, "You always take a big breath before you start speaking to an audience." So this was a method that I did instinctively. By taking that big breath, my first sentence was always strong and confident. Why? Because I had enough breath support.

My training as an actor taught me to have enough breath (and oxygen) to support what I was saying.

Some people run out of breath in the middle of a sentence, especially when they're nervous at the beginning of a speech.

The truth is I have felt nervous at the beginning of a speech, but with a big breath before speaking, I did *not* appear nervous.

I watch my audience members' faces. I know that when I begin with a deep breath and a strong first sentence, the audience feels they are in good hands.

I feel confident that I have begun well.

7. Energize a *good-pattern* before you're under stress

When I say "good-pattern," I'm talking about taking action in ways that build connection with the person or people you're talking with. But this requires preparation and practice.

I recommend putting your efforts into the good-pattern *before* you're under stress because people default to their conditioning when they're under stress (as noted in research studies). So you need to condition yourself to the good-pattern you want to exhibit. Here's another way of looking at it: "energize a good-pattern" means "choose excellent training."

I do not often refer to military principles, but this one is particularly useful in our current discussion: *More sweat in training; less blood in battle.*

Here are two Good-Patterns that you'll do well to prepare and practice:

a) Gentle Questions

These are questions that are easy-to-answer. They're positive in nature and invite conversation.

- "What's working for you at this conference?"
- "Which speaker are you looking forward to?"
- "What do you like about this association?"

b) Reflective Replies

When I say "Reflective Replies," I'm using the metaphor of a pool that reflects the image of a person. You function like a reflective pool as you assure the person that you're listening deeply and picking up what they're feeling.

- "That sounds frustrating."
- "That sounds painful. How did you keep going?"

To energize a good-pattern, first make a choice to train yourself or get training. Second, before you're in a stressful situation (like a job interview), rehearse. When you're in the stressful situation, use your training. Finally, after the stressful event, analyze how you did and adjust your subsequent rehearsal before the next time you face similar stressful conditions.

Excellent training and rehearsal fortify our feelings of confidence. We feel confident that we're as ready as we can be.

One last note: Choosing to train and rehearse is a keystone to personal freedom.

Your true freedom rests on your choice of your own programming. – Tom Marcoux

8. Notice and improve your posture

Imagine that there is a string going through your spine and pulling up to the ceiling. And picture that all of your vertebrae line up. You are not arching your back. You are, instead, aligning your vertebrae. I learned from three physical therapists (during my recovery from a car accident) that when you align your vertebrae, you actually expend less energy than when you slouch. How is that possible? When you slouch, your muscles have to hold you up. But your back was designed to hold you up with ease—when your vertebrae are aligned.

In addition, when you hold yourself with good posture, you look strong, confident, and competent. And you feel better. Other people pick up this vibe from you. They treat you better, which reinforces your feelings of confidence.

9. Target "If you're afraid, rehearse"

When you really want to live on a more exciting and fulfilling level, you're going to be stretching and growing—and entering situations that are new to you.

For over a decade, I have coached clients and graduate/college students in the skills of excellent public speaking. They memorize a phrase: "If you're afraid, rehearse."

Think of it. If you're feeling nervous, you're already uncomfortable. Imagine putting that energy to work by rehearsing. I've rehearsed before job interviews and even before stepping up to meet a celebrity at an event. Whether I was to meet best-selling authors like Guy Kawasaki, Chip Conley, Debbie Ford and others . . . or entertainers/actors like Dionne Warwick and George Takei (of *Star Trek* fame), I rehearsed. After all, it would do me no good to get tongue-tied when I met them. Instead, I knew ahead of time what I wanted to say concisely, and I was sure that I had chosen words that I could easily express.

Why rehearse? To create a *New Choice Conditioned Response*, which is your desired action in a given situation. The process includes the following steps:

a) you make a deliberate choice to create a new behavior.

b) you rehearse the desired behavior.

c) under a stressful or at least critical situation, you implement the desired behavior.

In other words: **You make a Cool Decision before a Hot Event.**

I describe this as: you make a careful choice of behavior before you experience the stressful situation.

I learned the value of creating my own New Choice Conditioned Response when I studied acting and had to learn numerous lines for a play. I came up with my own method. I recorded the play using different voices (impersonating other actors), and then I left empty spaces so that I would be able to respond with my lines. In essence, the other actors' lines served as "triggers" for my responding line of dialogue. In essence, I conditioned (trained) myself to respond to the trigger-lines of dialogue with my lines spoken by the character I was portraying.

Rehearsal, to me, is part of a process I call the *Trigger-Set Method* that I first introduced in my book *Nothing Can Stop You This Year!*

To feel confident, it often helps to identify triggers that will be present in the stressful environment that you will enter. Then you identify how you can train yourself (condition yourself) to take effective action.

Earlier I talked about how I take a deep breath before I say my first line of a speech. That's my own New Choice Conditioned Response. It supports my coming across as confident and competent.

The Trigger-Set Method in brief:
a) Identify a trigger to be present at the stressful event
b) Choose an empowering action.
c) Associate that empowering action with the trigger and rehearse that empowering action.
d) Implement that empowering action.

In addition, you can create your own positive trigger. For example, during a speech, a speaker can hold a Post-it note with her thumb and forefinger. This Post-it Note includes key words to serve as an outline for the speech. Holding that Post-it Note reassures her that she has something to fall back on if needed. This boosts her feelings of confidence.

Points to Remember:

P.I.E. for Confidence

Principle: Drop the idea that you need to feel comfortable to act like a confident person.

Inquiry: What would help you feel like you can adapt to whatever may come up in the stressful situation? How will you implement the methods for feeling confident?

Emotional Strength:
The essence of transformation is consistent rehearsal and creating your New Choice Conditioned Response.
What do you intend to use to strengthen your "feeling confident"?
Will you do some of the following?
a) Heart Breathing
b) Focus on "How are *you* doing?"
c) Identify "What would a confident person do?"
d) Find things to be impressed about in the person
e) Deep breathe before you speak
f) Energize a good-pattern before you're under stress
g) Improve your posture
h) Use the process, "If you're afraid, rehearse"

CHAPTER TWO:
THE P.E.R.S.U.A.D.E. PROCESS OF PERSUASION

When I recorded the audio program *The Best Kept Secrets of Masters of Persuasion*, I focused on observing and relating effective methods of people who have accomplished much — in other words — people who have changed the world.

This section shares secrets to help you
- Learn the Skills of the Best Persuaders including Oprah, US Presidents, Walt Disney, Anthony Robbins, Jesus, Gandhi, Mary Kay Ash, George Lucas, and many others
- Influence People to Follow Your Suggestions
- Easily Close Sales Faster
- Influence Family and Friends to Live in Healthy Ways

We'll use the P.E.R.S.U.A.D.E. process:

P – power up emotions
E – encourage team-energy
R – realize connection

S – seize attention
U – use language powerfully
A – act as a trusted advisor
D – do your preparation
E – energize yourself as a "coach-to-action"

In this section, you'll learn to gain trust faster and persuade people with ease.

An interviewer once asked me: "What's one of the most important things to know about persuasion?"

I replied, "When we talk about persuasion, we are talking about something ethical and appropriate. We are talking about something I call 'coaching-to-action.' What does a coach do?"

The interviewer replied, "A coach helps get you to do what you want to do."

That's it exactly. That's why I talk about *coaching-to-action* as related with persuasion. When you persuade, you start with a benefit for the person you're talking with.

Dictionary.com defines *persuasion* as "communication intended to induce belief or action."

I take that a step further: In persuasion, you focus on a benefit for the person you are talking with.

I want to be absolutely clear that I'm talking about persuasion as a *positive* process.

This is in contrast to manipulation, which is pulling strings only for selfish reasons.

Dictionary.com defines *manipulation* as "exerting shrewd or devious influence especially for one's own advantage."

In a few words the difference is:

Persuasion is helping.
Manipulation is selfish and pulling strings.

In this section, the person you want to persuade is

someone we will call the listener.

I'll refer to you as the *effective persuader*.

1. Power Up Emotions

When her show was still in production, Oprah Winfrey made it fun to be an audience member on her show (certainly during the holiday season). Making things fun can energize your persuasion efforts. So can being genuine.

In the first class, every semester, of my public speaking class, I share with college students: *"We don't need you to be perfect; we do need you to be genuine."*

Oprah definitely had *genuine* compassion going for her. The audience knew of her childhood journey with abuse, and they could see true emotion on Oprah's face. This helped Oprah make a genuine connection with her audience.

One reason so few of us achieve what we truly want is that we never direct our focus; we never concentrate our power. Most people dabble their way through life, never deciding to master anything in particular. – Anthony Robbins

Along the lines of Anthony Robbins' comment, I invite you to put forth real effort and to concentrate on inspiring positive emotions in the listener.

One way to power up positive emotions is to demonstrate that you're giving your full attention. I call this process *Heart-Faces-Heart*. When you speak with someone, make sure that you are facing them. I use the phrase heart-faces-heart as a quick reminder.

Why is this important? Many times, if we stand with our feet facing away, on the subconscious level, people may feel that we really want to run away. Joe Navarro, ex-FBI agent and author of *What Every Body Is Saying,* emphasizes that agents are trained to assess whether someone is telling the truth by first looking at their feet, then hands, and finally face.

Many people may keep their face impassive, but their feet and hands give them away.

My point is that when you focus on Heart-Faces-Heart and you align your chest to face the other person, your feet naturally follow. You body comes into alignment. You appear to be giving full attention to the listener.

In this discussion of Power Up Emotions, let's remember, too, that when people are being persuaded, what they are buying is energy. We want them to buy the perception that we're good people, and we want them to feel good in our company.

Susan RoAnne, author of *How to Work a Room*, said simply, "Be fun." She employs that in her own speaking and writing. She uses Yiddish words like *chutzpah* and original titles like *Conversensations*.

Consider Using Humor—But Be Careful

Laughter is the shortest distance between two people.
– Victor Borge

US President Ronald Reagan persuaded a nation and the media to drop the issue of his age. In 1984 during a presidential debate, his opponent, Walter Mondale brought up Ronald Reagan's age of 73. And Reagan responded: "I want you to know that also I will not make age an issue of this campaign. I am not going to exploit, for political purposes, my opponent's youth and inexperience."

The audience laughed, and even Mondale admitted that Reagan's comment scored well.

Speaking of US Presidents, I had the opportunity hear in-person President Bill Clinton. As a member of private luncheon group of 273 people, I appreciated his sharing secrets of giving speeches. He emphasized the power of using the microphone so that one comes across as friendly and comfortable. "It puts everyone at ease," he explained.

His charisma was impressive. He also said, "I've seen that most people who are bitter have not known catastrophes. *I've* known catastrophes." His tone got the audience laughing with him.

Among various attributes, US Presidents share a distinction: "They're the greatest networkers in the world." (noted Harvey Mackay, author of *Swim with the Sharks Without Getting Eaten Alive*)

Here is a crucial technique Bill Clinton used to get elected. Every day he went over 3x5 index cards of people he met that day. He memorized personal details. When someone knows your son's name, you are likely to warm up to that person. *This powers up emotion.*

Special Element of Power Up Emotions . . . Influence the Influencers

People don't make decisions by themselves. Think about the folks who may affect [the person's] decisions.
– Guy Kawasaki

Realize to guide a person to make a favorable decision, you're not only influencing the listener, but you're also in better stead to influence his or her influencers. Years ago, comedian Bill Cosby said, "If a man thinks he rules the castle, let him buy drapes by himself." Cosby's comment identified the power of the man's wife.

Marketing data identifies that women influence 85% of all purchases. A similar finding states "Women account for 85% of all consumer purchases including everything from autos to health care."

MassMutual Financial Group identified that "Senior women age 50 and older control net worth of $19 trillion and own more than three-fourths of the nation's financial wealth."

Here is more salient data:

- Women make 80% of healthcare decisions and 68 percent of new car purchase decisions
- 75% of women identified themselves as the primary shoppers for their households
- Women influenced $90 billion of consumer electronic purchases in 2007
- Women account for 58% of all total online spending
- 22% of women shop online at least once a day
- 92% of women pass along information about deals or finds to others

(sources: She-Economy, Ms Smith Marketing, StartUpNation, Clickz, Inc.com, Girl Power Marketing, Catalyst, Forbes)

As we talk about the concept of influencing the influencers, let's take a second look at the statistic "92% of women pass along information about deals or finds to others."

Marketers and other persuaders had better pay close attention to women making purchase decisions and influencing others' purchase decisions.

In summary, directly appeal to the influencers of your listener. In other words, get the influencer to like you and trust you.

If you sell a high ticket item, invite the listener to allow you to address their influencer in a further meeting. The truth is your listener may agree with you in the showroom, but their influencer at home (or a consultant like an accountant or lawyer) may easily talk them out of purchasing what you offer.

Do *not* fall for this situation. Be sure to directly interact with your listeners' influencers. And remember to power up emotions.

Points to Remember:

Principle #1: Power Up Emotions

Power Questions:
How can you engage your listener's emotions? What will move the person to take action in the direction you want? Who influences the listener? How can you interact directly with the influencer (a spouse, accountant, lawyer, or other person)?

* * * * * *

2. Encourage Team-Energy

By team-energy, I mean that you get the person to feel a connection to you and what you're talking about.

This brings us back to two processes we covered earlier in this book: a) Soft-Hearted Persuasion and b) Warm Trust Charisma.

In Soft-Hearted Persuasion, you metaphorically walk over to the listener's position, and together you look at the listener's problem.

In Warm Trust Charisma, you do two things: You extend

your hand in friendship, and you get obstacles out of your way to making a warm connection.

For example, Frank Bettger, author of *How I Raised Myself from Failure to Success in Selling*, suggested that you get a customer to participate in a demonstration. If you can do that, then on a subconscious level, you and the customer have formed a team. You're working together. You're not at different sides of the desk. You're standing on the same side, looking outward toward the problem.

Further, I have used this process when introducing my feature film projects. I had a meeting with a top attorney at a major firm in Los Angeles. Instead of sitting down across from the attorney, I moved my chair to the side of the person's desk. In this way, we looked at my materials together. I was not across from her. We were on the same side. I had the binder available, and she could turn pages at her own speed.

The #1 real estate agent for Century 21 is a friendly, effective woman named Marty Rodriguez. When I interviewed her, she told me how she turned her business into a 100% referral business. From the beginning of her career, she went the extra mile to be helpful to people. When you're helpful to other people, then people start to feel like one team or one family. Marty told me about the time one of her clients who was selling a home suddenly experienced vandalism. The older woman called up Marty, who quickly sent her husband to help clean up the mess. Marty was a living example of the old adage: A good salesperson is a professional friend.

The Role of "Identity" in Team-Energy

Identity has two roles in the persuasion process:

a) The listener's preferred identity for herself or himself

c) Your identity as a team member to the listener (to accomplish the listener's goals)

The Listener's Preferred Identity

Authors Matthew W. Ragas and BJ Bueno, in their book, *The Power of Cult Branding*, wrote ". . . thousands of Mac users show up at computer stores and other public places all the time, for free, to evangelize about Apple's products and their love of the Mac. . . . Today, the Harley [Harley-Davidson] logo can be found not only on its legendary chrome-covered motorcycles, but on everything from clothing (MotorClothes) like jackets, T-shirts, jeans, and panties to off-beat items like Harley-branded leather toilet seat coves, playing cards, wall clocks, and coffee mugs. HD also operates Harley-Davidson Cafe . . . in Las Vegas."

One reader at Amazon.com wrote: "All of the brands featured in the book facilitate people getting together so they can go and be with their 'own kind.' At these events, customers of these brands can form extended families that share in the same value system as they do. It's a practical guide to how a company can help and reward their loyal customers by supporting them, by helping the customer to achieve fulfillment in their lives. Take Harley, for example, they host bike week events and support bike clubs; Vans Shoes, they build skate parks; Jimmy Buffet, he does music that strikes a chord with people of many different backgrounds and they form groups who support and help each other."

Oprah Winfrey's TV shows, OWN (cable network), and her magazine *O* revolve around an idea summarized with the catchphrase at Oprah's web site: "Live Your Best Life" By partaking of Oprah's programs/products, a fan subconsciously agrees that she's aiming to live her best life.

Your Identity as a Team Member to the Listener

Earlier, I wrote of an effective salesperson as a "coach-to-action." To have this identity, you need to develop competence, self-esteem, and warmth because your listener will pick up on whether you radiate "I'm here to help you and you can trust that I know what I'm doing and what I talk about."

Mary Kay Ash built a multimillion dollar organization, Mary Kay Cosmetics, through the power of team-building and developing the "ideal identity" in her Mary Kay Independent Beauty Consultants.

Before I go further, I'll share how big this process has become. Mary Kay Inc., one of the largest direct sellers of skin care and color cosmetics in the world, often tops $1.6 billion in annual wholesale sales. The company's independent sales force includes nearly 1.3 million Mary Kay Independent Beauty Consultants in more than 30 markets worldwide. Mary Kay Inc. has averaged double-digit annual growth since the company's founding in 1963 and celebrates 50 years of enriching women's lives. The secret to this success is that Mary Kay helped the women who started with her company.

It was about feeling part of a team—and it was about having an Ideal Identity to strive for.

Mary Kay Ash built up the new women's self-esteem and capabilities. Let's explore some of her focus points embodied in her words:

- "There are two things people want more than sex and money... recognition and praise.
- No matter how busy you are, you must take time to make the other person feel important.
- We treat our people like royalty. If you honor and serve the people who work for you, they will honor and serve you.

• A mediocre idea that generates enthusiasm will go farther than a great idea that inspires no one."

Mary Kay Inc. has been famous for taking in shy women who were too nervous to order a pizza via the phone and nurturing them to become top money-earning consultants.

So, how did Mary Kay Ash get many timid women to sell so many cosmetics?

Based on my observations of published accounts, I see three key reasons:

a) There was a fun and nurturing environment.

Sales meetings were full of applause, humor, and encouragement.

b) There were clear rewards.

Women earned, not only monetary awards, but also acclaim. Top earners would be presented awards with big applause and music and celebration. Mary Kay would say, "Are you ready for the most exciting moment in your life?"

c) There was a series of levels to climb and achieve.

Mary Kay was famous for awarding pink Cadillac cars to her top earners.

Give yourself something to work toward—constantly. – Mary Kay Ash

In summary, there are some significant observations about team-energy.

• Get the listener involved in a demonstration.

• Use Soft-Hearted Persuasion, ask questions, and give the listener the subconscious impression that you're going over to her position and that together you're looking at her problem.

• Be aware of the importance of "Identity."

- Develop your own identity as a competent and warm "team member to the listener."

As I review the effectiveness of the Mary Kay process, I realize that enthusiasm is a big factor. Steven Spielberg also uses enthusiasm to lead team members. He says, "A good director knows when to say 'yes.'"

Actor Ben Kingsley (co-star in Spielberg's film *Schindler's List*) talked about how exciting it was hearing Spielberg's enthusiastic, "That's going to be in the movie!"

In conclusion, demonstrate that you're on the listener's side and that you're enthusiastic about how your offering will help the person.

Points to Remember:

Principle #2: Encourage Team-Energy

Power Questions:
How can you do a demonstration in which the listener participates? How can you make the situation feel like you're on the same team, on the same side, looking outward at the problem?

* * * * * *

3. Realize Connection

When I write "realize connection," I'm talking about two things: a) you already have forms of connection with someone and b) you can enhance your connection with the person.

You already have forms of connection with someone.

When you listen intently, you inspire a person to feel valued. That's a good start for connection. One way that we easily connect is in the fact that we all feel pain. Expressing empathy for the other person's difficulties emphasizes connection and often creates a form of camaraderie.

You can enhance your connection with the person.

You improve the listener's sense of connection with you when you express how you share common concerns, traits, and feelings. People tend to like those who seem similar to them. Researcher Robert Cialdini, author of the classic book *Influence*, noted that many people are influenced by people whom they like and appreciate. So as an effective persuader, you need to show that similarity, that connection.

Ultimately, we want the listener to realize the connection with you—human being to human being.

A simple way to help the person feel connected to you

David Barron, persuasion expert and co-author of *Power Persuasion*, emphasizes that it helps to say "I agree." When you say "I agree," it puts the other person at ease.

Being Genuine: The Way to Make a Real Connection

Mahatma Gandhi greeted a mother and son who had travelled many miles to receive guidance. The mother was worried and asked Gandhi, "Please tell my son to stop eating sugar." Gandhi gently replied, "Come back in one week."

The mother listened and returned with her son one week later. Then Gandhi simply turned to the boy and said, "Stop eating sugar."

"Why did you have us travel so far?" the mother asked.

"Last week, I was eating sugar," Gandhi replied.

Happiness is when what you think, what you say, and what you do are in harmony. – Mahatma Gandhi

Gandhi demonstrated that one can be influential when one demonstrates personal integrity.

We need to be consistent. We need to be genuine.

Learn a Secret for Persuading from Joe Vitale . . . The power of the "Hypnotic Story"

When I spoke with Joe Vitale (an author highlighted in *The Secret*, a book with more than 19 million copies sold), he said, "My favorite [persuasion technique] is a hypnotic story about someone who used my product or service and benefited from it. The story goes under the conscious radar and communicates and persuades without objection."

Here is an example of how Joe used an effective story:

****Below is a Portion of Joe's Email Message to his e-subscribers list*****

Just released - "Spiritual Marketing In Action"
http://www.spiritualmarketinginaction.com

If you are in the helping or healing profession---if you are a coach, counselor, therapist, hypnotist, or any number of people who help or heal people--the following news is for you. (If this isn't for you, please forward this to who you think will want it.)

Best-selling author, self-help pioneer, and legendary speaker Dr. Robert Anthony once told me--

"I will tell you up front, if you are not overwhelmed with clients or customers, something is wrong. This may make you uncomfortable, but if paying clients aren't lined up for your products or services the ONLY reason is because YOU are the one keeping them from your door."

And he's right.

Because I know Dr. Anthony, and because he knows my books on marketing, we teamed up to write an entire manual to help people in the helping and healing professions get more clients.

It's called "Spiritual Marketing In Action."

You can read all about it at--

http://www.spiritualmarketinginaction.com

It's one of the greatest joys of my life to have experienced working with the great Dr. Anthony in creating a method to help YOU.

Again, this material is only for those who are looking for more clients. If that isn't you, please pass this message to someone you think may welcome it.

****End of the Above Portion of Joe Vitale's Email to his e-subscribers list****

Let's break down the key elements of Joe's email message:

1) An instant connection to certain readers: "If you are in the helping or healing profession---if you are a coach, counselor, therapist, hypnotist, or any number of people who help or heal people--the following news is for you." Joe is aware that a number of people in the helping professions feel distaste for marketing, so he makes it palatable with "spiritual marketing."

2) Instant Credibility from Quoting A Renowned Expert in the Field: "Best-selling author, self-help pioneer, and legendary speaker Dr. Robert Anthony" When people encounter any form of message they have certain questions: a) Who are you? and b) Why should I listen to you? Quoting an authority provides answers to both questions.

3) A message directed toward "you": "I will tell you up front, if you are not overwhelmed with clients or customers, something is wrong. This may make you uncomfortable, but if paying clients aren't lined up for your products or services the ONLY reason is because YOU are the one keeping them from your door." The word *you* basically takes hold of the reader like grabbing his or her collar and saying, "Pay attention to this."

4) Instant connection to the reader's desire: "Again, this material is only for those who are looking for more clients." Call out the reader's desire and you have their attention. They likely have a subconscious thought: "I better focus on this. I might be able to get what I really want!"

Joe Vitale has earned millions of dollars through developing and using his skills of connection.

Persuasion arises from connection.

Points to Remember:

Principle #3: Realize Connection

Power Questions:
How can you help the listener know that you have common concerns, traits, and feelings? How can you tell an "hypnotic story"?

* * * * * *

4. Seize attention

Just imagine how much competition for a person's attention is going on at any given moment. Many of us are entranced by our smart phones, computers, video games, televisions, and more.

As an effective persuader, you must compete with a lot of noise. So do something to appropriately seize the person's attention and make what you're talking about clear. For example, George Lucas used paintings to get *Star Wars* placed with 20th Century Fox studio. George had an idea of Darth Vader in his mind. He conveyed the idea to artist Ralph McQuarie, and soon Alan Ladd, Jr., president of 20th Century Fox, was able to see and feel the idea through the paintings. George Lucas said, "Dreams are extremely important. You can't do it unless you imagine it."

Walt Disney wanted his laborers to really understand that, with Disneyland, they were working on something magical, so he told them, "Build the castle first." You could imagine some of the workers turning to one another and saying, "Wow! Isn't that something? I want to bring my kids here."

Further, Walt Disney ran out of funds for completing his first animated feature film, *Snow White and the Seven Dwarfs*. So he gathered loan officers of Bank of America to see some footage. He also acted out all the characters. It's been said that one of the loan officers had tears in his eyes and said, "Give him the money."

How do you seize attention? For over a decade, I have taught elements of writing science fiction and fantasy story and screenplay writing on the college and graduate school levels. I mention what I call the *3 Elements of a Good Beginning:* a startling image, a dramatic question, and salting phrases. These 3 Elements can help you seize attention:

A Startling Image

For the cover of my book *Darkest Secrets of Business Communication: How to Protect Yourself and Command Your Personal Brand to Save Time, Reduce Stress and Make More*

Money, I had a startling image created: A hand reaches out of a computer monitor to pull a credit card from a guy's wallet while he's looking away from the screen. For various projects, I tend to test two compelling images. On an airplane, I might turn to another passenger in the seat next to me and say, "I'm curious. Which one of these possible covers would get you to pick up a book for you or a friend?" I show two compelling images. (I call this *Choice Market Testing*.)

A Dramatic Question

"What is going on here? Why did he do that?" Inspiring a question in someone's mind can gain their attention. For example, I have demonstrated this principle by rolling a quarter across a desk while my graduate students look on. Soon I ask them: "What question arose in your mind?"

To seize someone's attention, see if you can arouse some experience of suspense. For instance, I once started a section of a speech with:

"So I'm doing my own stunt. I'm hanging by my finger tips on the front of a classic Chevy truck going 50 miles an hour. I was not thinking about the cameraman's shot. I was really concerned about . . ."

What was I really concerned about? So now we have a dramatic question.

Salting Phrases

You likely recall an old phrase: "You can lead a horse to water but you can't make him drink—*unless you salt his oats first.*" (the italicized idea suggested by author Steven Scott). When I say "salting phrase," I mean you say something that makes the listener thirsty to hear what you say next.

Here's an example:

"There was one thing that Lynda Obst—she produced *Sleepless In Seattle* with Tom Hanks—told me about getting attention in a Hollywood meeting. Would you like to hear her technique?"

That's a salting phrase.

The Power of a Story

Simply express a new idea, and you'll likely get resistance. But tell a story, and you can give the person an experience that she'll remember. For over a decade I have taught Comparative Religion on the college level. I have noted that Jesus of Nazareth seized the attention of listeners through powerful stories known as parables. Part of the power of a parable is that the audience can see the situation in their mind's eye. For example, in the *Parable of the Mustard Seed* in *Matthew* Chapter 13, Jesus conveys an idea vividly:

"The same day went Jesus out of the house, and sat by the sea side. And great multitudes were gathered together unto him, so that he went into a ship, and sat; and the whole multitude stood on the shore. And he spake many things unto them in parables, saying, "Behold, a sower went forth to sow. And when he sowed, some seeds fell by the way side, and the fowls came and devoured them up. Some fell upon stony places, where they had not much earth and forthwith they sprung up, because they had no deepness of earth. And when the sun was up, they were scorched; and because they had no root, they withered away. And some fell among thorns; and the thorns sprung up, and choked them: But other fell into good ground, and brought forth fruit, some an hundredfold, some sixtyfold, some thirtyfold."

The listeners of this parable can picture the various situations and feel the concluding idea of a seed falling into good ground and yielding a substantial harvest.

Energize the Listener's Emotional Brain

The emotional brain focuses on preventing loss. Paul McKenna and Michael Breen, the authors of *The Power to Influence*, seize attention by using a scary approach. They advertise their audio program by saying that methods of influence (discussed in their program) are being used on you—and that you can learn to protect yourself from unwanted influences. This Scary Approach seizes attention. Use this technique carefully because some people will resent being pushed in this manner.

Martin Luther King, Jr. was a master of seizing attention. He held his demonstration in Birmingham, Alabama. It is reported that he knew that it was likely that violent resistance to his peaceful demonstrators would take place and such horrible images would be powerful on television.

Martin Luther King, Jr. also has seized the attention of people for decades now with his "I have a dream" speech. He didn't say, "I've got a well-thought out management strategy for consumer buy-in."

No, he said, *I have a dream* . . . "I have a dream that my four children will one day live in a nation where they will not be judged by the color of their skin but by the content of their character. I have a dream today."

Seizing Attention Often Occurs When Taking Some Form of Appropriate Risk

Jay Abraham is a master of marketing. He has coached Anthony Robbins, considered one of the most financially successful speakers in history.

Jay Abraham said, "If you truly believe that what you have is useful and valuable to your clients, then you have a moral obligation to try to serve them in every way possible."

Abraham certainly believes in the value of his work, and

he *took a risk* by using a startling way to advertise one of his audio programs. He included an *unusual* quote from Vic Conant of the Nightingale-Conant Company: "Jay Abraham irritates me. He is brash. And at the same time, Jay gets results. One idea from Jay resulted in a $900,000 in flow of cash into Nightingale-Conant Company."

So the implication is that it's worth it, to put up with Jay, because *Jay Gets Results.*

To have any chance of persuading someone, you need to seize attention first.

Points to Remember:

Principle #4: Seize Attention

Power Questions:
How can you seize attention? What makes you different? What kind of effective story can you tell?

* * * * * *

5. Use language powerfully

Have you noticed that certain words inspire images and feelings?

The Power of a Word Picture
Years ago, I wanted to convey how painful it was to be waiting for my then-girlfriend:

"When I'm waiting for you, I'm like a puppy on a raft in the middle of the Atlantic ocean, never knowing if a rescue boat is coming."

Recently, a college student in my public speaking class asked, "Did it work?"

I replied, "Yes. Or I wouldn't mention it."

The "puppy on a raft" phrase is called a Word Picture. Using word pictures is part of employing language in a powerful way.

Powerful Language Avoids Raising Disruptive Fear

Tom Hopkins, author of *How to Master the Art of Selling*, emphasized how the words "sign here" raise fear. Some people immediately think of "signing my life away." Hopkins' solution was to invite the customer to "okay this."

Hopkins also had a substitution for "when you buy this"; he suggested saying, "When you're enjoying the benefits of . . ." If you say "buy," the person may become fearful with an idea like: "Oh no, if I buy this, I won't be able to recover if I've made a mistake."

On the other hand, "When you're enjoying the benefits of . . ." encourages the person to feel positive feelings and to anticipate feeling empowered while using the product or service. Here's another useful substitution for "buy": "When you own this . . ."

Help Customers Feel Their Way Through

Be careful of the word "why." Often when customers answer a "Why do you---?" question, they feel placed on the defensive. They jump into their head and make things up. They make up rationalizations for their behaviors or previously held thoughts. People do like to appear consistent.

Substitute the word "how" for "why." Say something like: "So how does that work for you?" Or "How do you see yourself using [this product]?"

You can use Appropriate Fear

Have you noticed that many of us really go into action to prevent a situation that we fear? That phenomenon inspires me to use the phrase "appropriate fear." Some things require us to take action and prepare. For instance, if you are travelling to certain countries, it is an appropriate concern (or "appropriate fear") for your health to identify which inoculations and bug repellants to obtain and which procedures about local water to focus on.

This type of fear is different from the "disruptive fear" I spoke of earlier, and it can be useful to appeal to customers' sense of caution.

If you really want them to feel the value of your product or service, you could use the word "what." You could ask, "What would you lose if you don't get this product today?"

Effective Ways to Say "Wonder" and "Why"

You could say, "I wonder how we can take care of the details and make sure you don't miss this opportunity—before the deadline." The word wonder, used in this way, can be a mild and friendly way to guide a conversation.

Although I often avoid asking "why" when enticing a person to consider some product or service, I've noticed that I can use "why" for a particular situation. If the person seems on the fence about deciding to get one of my products, I mildly ask, "Why don't you take it?" Many times, they're startled, and then . . . they nod to themselves and purchase my product.

Identify the Importance of Word Choice and Nonverbal Elements of Your Message

One interviewer asked me, "So you're saying that specific words work better than others. I have heard that words are only 7% of the message and that 38% is vocal and 55% is visual (what people see)." I replied, "Well, the point we need to look at is making the body language and the visual match the words. If you see someone breaking the top off a chair and saying 'I'm not angry,' the words and the visual are not lining up."

The point about words is that you, the effective persuader, be comfortable.

Your comfort will flow to the listener, creating the listener's comfort and openness to your influence.

Points to Remember:

Principle #5: Use Language Powerfully

Power Questions:
How can you use words to connect with the person's emotions? What words would help you? What words do you feel are ones to drop from your conversations?

* * * * * *

6. Act as a trusted advisor

Trust is a precious thing. Some people have inspired a vast number of people to trust them. For example, Mother Theresa's trustworthiness inspired people to join her efforts when she founded the Missionaries of Charity. Many people participated with over 4,000 sisters, an associated brotherhood of 300 members, and over 100,000 lay volunteers—all operating 610 missions in 123 countries. These included hospices and homes for people with HIV/AIDS, leprosy, and tuberculosis. The 610 missions provided soup kitchens, children's and family counseling programs, orphanages, and schools.

For some people, Mother Theresa was a controversial figure. However, Mother Theresa (winner of the Nobel Peace Prize in 1979) was persuasive about her mission. To be trusted . . . it is about the stories you tell. And the stories that are told about you. When people heard that Mother Teresa only had two saris, they knew that their contributions to her work were going to go to the poorest of the poor . . . and not to anyone's big salary.

Mother Teresa was genuine. She said, "I won't walk in a march against war. But if you have a march *for* peace, I will walk in that."

Becoming a Trusted Advisor

To be the trusted advisor, follow Mother Teresa's advice: "Let no one come to you without leaving better."

To act as a trusted advisor, you need to develop your skills. Think of skill development as somewhat similar to developing muscle if you were doing weight training. Along this line, 2004 winner of the Nobel prize, researcher Richard Axel said that for violinists, the part of their brain that propels the pinky finger is three to five times bigger than that of the average person. This is a demonstration of the plasticity of the brain.

For the brain to develop so well, we're talking about taking massive action. (Think of the massive amounts of practice performed by a top level violinist.)

Along this line, we've hear the old question: "How do you get to Carnegie Hall?" And the answer is: "Practice, practice, practice."

What do you practice?

To Be Trusted, Be Impeccable About Keeping Agreements

This next idea comes from the multimillionaire Jack

Canfield, the co-creator of the *Chicken Soup for the Soul* series of books and more. Jack is also the co-author of *The Success Principles*.

Jack says: "Keep Your Agreements."

He points out that people who don't keep agreements lose trust, respect, and credibility with customers, friends, and family.

Jack offers these tips about keeping your agreements:

1) make only agreements you intend to keep
2) write down all the agreements you make
3) communicate any broken agreement at the first appropriate time
4) learn to say "no" more often

The third tip "communicate any broken agreement at the first appropriate time" can be interpreted as "tell the person that something prevents you from keeping your commitment as soon as you can."

My point here is that to persuade effectively you must be seen as trustworthy and credible.

Jack Canfield emphasizes that you need to be a "Class Act."

Points to Remember:

Principle #6: Act as a Trusted Advisor

Power Questions:

How can you help people see you as trustworthy? What small promise can you make and then definitely come through on?

* * * * * *

7. Do your preparation

I often say, "Courage is easier when you're prepared."
What does that mean?

First, prepare. Yes, you know what that means. It's like your teachers told you: "Do your homework." In other words, do your research, and then review, study, and practice what you've learned.

Second, with such preparation, you'll be ready to push yourself through fear to get important things done. You'll have the knowledge, tools, and new capabilities to stretch yourself and create success and fulfillment.

Preparation is an important, foundational element of Soft-Hearted Persuasion (mentioned earlier). In order to serve a potential client or even to help a friend, you need to think through how your offering might be of service.

You want to prepare a buffet table of benefits so that the person can identify what's most important to him or her. There are two elements to this process.

The first element is to get to know your product so well that you know the value it provides. You talk with previous buyers. You get testimonials.

The second element is to think deeply about the prospective buyer's situation. For example, Fred Bettger, the author of *How I Raised Myself from Failure to Success in Selling*, wrote of how he helped a business man protect his business. Mr. Booth was shopping around for life insurance so that he could borrow $250,000. His creditors insisted that he have life insurance to cover that $250,000.

In helping his prospective client, Fred Bettger did his preparation and realized what was the most vulnerable point for Mr. Booth: he needed to take his medical exam as fast as possible or maybe something would show up on the exam that would cancel the life insurance. That would cancel the $250,000 line of credit, and then Booth's business would be in trouble.

So Fred set up a medical exam for the very day he met Mr. Booth. He explained what really was at stake with Mr. Booth's delays in choosing an insurance provider.

This was the secret of Fred's successful persuasion. Fred found the most important detail, which was to make sure that Mr. Booth gained his $250,000 line of credit and did not miss his chance.

Fred focused on two important questions:

a) What is the key issue?

b) What is the client's most vulnerable point [and how can I help]?

Crucial Preparation: Create Your Effective Personal Brand

A quick way to get to the essence of a personal brand is to imagine saying:

- This is who I am.
- This is what you can count on me to do.
- This is evidence that I am trustworthy.

My favorite way to start working with your personal brand is to focus on answering this question:

What are you best known for?

This question is emphasized by Lois P. Frankel, author of *Nice Girls Don't Get the Corner Office.*

The truth is: You already have a personal brand right now. The question is: Is it the personal brand that you want?

For example, I have a friend who has *not* been on time for any social occasion in seven years. When this person applied to work with my company, I necessarily said there was no opening. The personal brand of "always late" was not helpful to this applicant.

Here are better personal brands:
- "You can rely on me to come up with a creative solution that protects the budget."
- "A team member coined the phrase 'Cost-cutting captain' when she talked about my strengths."
- "I'm known as being 'firm but fair.'"

Here is another definition of a personal brand:

Your Personal Brand is the powerful, clear, positive idea that comes to mind whenever other people think of you. It's what you stand for—the values, abilities and actions that others associate with you. . . . [It tells:] Who you are; What you do; What makes you different, or how you create value for your target market. – Peter Montoya

Pull out a sheet of paper and answer the questions posed above in the Peter Montoya's comment.

Prepare Before You Talk With a Prospective Client or Other Person

An important part of preparation is to review important personal details related to the person you will soon talk with. Later in this book, I describe in detail the "How I Can Help Plan." Using this process, you write down details about the person you have met and her family members. You include details like the person's hobbies, her family member's hobbies, college attended, and birthdays. Before you meet with the person, you do your preparation process: Review these details. Then you'll be able to warm up your upcoming interaction with her.

An important part of preparation is to focus on what the person really wants. Here is how Harvey MacKay, author of *Swim with the Sharks Without Getting Eaten Alive,* connected so well with TV talk show host Larry King that Harvey appeared on Larry King's show six times!

Harvey knew that Larry King had written books. And Harvey had special information to help Larry sell more books. First, Harvey suggested how Larry could get more of his books in bookstores. Ingram is the largest wholesaler of books. If Larry would go to Nashville and give a short speech to the 100-person sales force, those salespeople would talk up his book and place more books in bookstores.

Then Harvey talked about how he met the president of Barnes & Noble/B. Dalton. He told the president that he would be on a 35-city tour and would talk up their stores on every radio and TV show he was on. Harvey influenced him to increase the B. Dalton order from 1,500 to 15,000 copies of his book. Once he had achieved that, Harvey then went to Waldenbooks and asked why they were ordering a token amount of books when B. Dalton had ordered 15,000 copies. Seven days later Waldenbooks ordered 15,000 copies of Harvey's book.

The point here is that Harvey gave Larry King news he could use.

Harvey says, "In networking, you're only as good as what you give away."

How did Harvey get his special knowledge? Through preparation. He gave himself a six-month self-taught course on the publishing business. He did this by talking with 30 authors, many literary agents, 12 publishers, some promotional firms, and six lawyers. Talk about doing his homework!

A Special Note About Persuading Your Family Members and Friends to Live in Healthy Ways

A core principle of persuading is: "It does not matter

what you say; it matters what they say."

Much of your preparation is focused on asking non-threatening and non-coercive questions.

Earlier in this book, I mentioned the following process of asking questions.

Here is another sample of such a dialogue:

Gabriel: Damn! I wish I could stop smoking!
Sabrina: I hear you. How would you go about it?
Gabriel: That's just it. I've tried over and over again. Nothing works.
Sabrina: I'm curious. How ready are you to try to find new ways to stop the habit? On a scale of 1 to 10—ten means you're the most ready—how ready are you?
Gabriel: Oh – five.
Sabrina: Why didn't you say four?
Gabriel: I guess because I'm concerned that I might get lung cancer like Aunt Tina did. Also, there's this girl I'm interested in. Her name's Mary. I think she doesn't like smoking around her.

Remember, like Sabrina did with Gabriel, true persuasion occurs when you can elicit the other person's reasons—and when you avoid shoving your own reasons down his throat.

This is especially important when it comes to family and friends. Somehow we tend to resist most those closest to us.

So offer no opportunity for resistance. Just offer support for the person to find his or her reasons and personal power for change.

* * *

Preparation is truly a key toward effective persuasion.

Success always comes when preparation meets opportunity.
– Henry Hartman

Points to Remember:

Principle #7: Do Your Preparation

Power Questions:
How can you get yourself prepared? What expert tips or stories do you need to prepare so that you can say them smoothly and clearly—and briefly?

* * * * * *

8. Energize yourself as a "coach-to-action"

When you focus on being a "coach-to-action," you eliminate hesitation and procrastination in selling. Why? You're not pushing; you're helping.

Here's a summary of elements of being a coach-to-action:
a) find out how you can help the buyer
b) be perceived as an expert
c) be memorable
d) build on what the buyer already knows

Find out how you can help the buyer.
Top Coach Tom Landry said, "A coach is someone who tells you what you don't want to hear, who has you see what you don't want to see, so you can be who you have always known you could be." This is a powerful approach. Let's focus first on the part "So you can be who you have always known you could be." In essence, the coach "holds the space" for a person raise their performance level. The idea "holds

the space" relates to the concept is that one needs a place to put something. So when I say, "find out how you can help the buyer," I invite you to observe and communicate the positive potential of the buyer, which they can fulfill with your offering (product or service).

Be perceived as an expert.

When I met Dr. Richard Carlson, author of the *Don't Sweat the Small Stuff* series, we were both guests on a radio show. During a break, he pulled me aside and gave me coaching since he was further along as a speaker and author. I learned that he embodied his *Don't Sweat the Small Stuff* brand. He was warm, friendly, and comfortable. It was obvious that his methods were working in his own life.

Be memorable.

To form your messages as something memorable will take consistent effort and preparation. For example, Dr. John Gray developed the material that eventually became the best-seller *Men Are From Mars, Women Are From Venus*.

Gray wrote: "As I developed and taught the *Men Are From Mars* ideas in the eighties, many people became upset with me….For six years, few people were coming to my seminars…I felt the agony of not knowing and prayed to God to show me the way….Gradually it became clearer and clearer…I kept experiencing that the insights could actually save marriages….With every new insight, I thanked God."

Gray wrote other books including *What Your Mother Couldn't Tell You and Your Father Didn't Know: Advanced Relationship Skills for Better Communication and Lasting Intimacy*. He was on track, but it was not until he released *Men Are From Mars, Women Are From Venus* that his message became memorable.

How do you make your message memorable? Use what I call *Choice Market Testing*. For example, sometimes when on a plane, I'll turn to a nearby passenger and show two potential covers of a book and ask:

- "Which book looks like one you'd consider for yourself or a friend?"
- "What about [your choice] grabs your attention?"

I listen carefully to the person's responses. Then with a team member, I discuss possible improvements for the cover.

Build on what the buyer already knows.

Buyers know that doctors study for several years. They hold doctors in high esteem. Deepak Chopra, MD has built upon this premise. He's known as a medical doctor who has conducted research. Further, he went to India to study two-thousand-year-old wisdom known as ayurvedic medicine.

Chopra begins with credibility as a medical doctor; then he touches on quantum physics—then topics about how all of our cells have a "type of wisdom." He continues into spiritual topics. Numerous readers and audience members are willing to go with Chopra because he already has credibility and they know it.

How a Coach-to-Action Supports the "Team-Focused Person"

You can often coach someone to action if the benefit is for someone else. Parents will often do more for their children than for themselves. They will work harder and sacrifice more out of love for their children. I've coined the term "Team-Focused Person" to describe someone who will do more for another person than the self.

I learned a secret of persuasion from Benjamin Franklin. In his autobiography, Ben Franklin wrote about how he raised funds for public libraries—from wealthy citizens—when he emphasized the benefits for other people. Public libraries have served communities for decades. For example, millionaire and author Brian Tracy reported that when he had little funds, he studied books on real estate that he borrowed from the library.

You can improve your consistency as an effective persuader when you use the paradigm of the coach-to-action.

Points to Remember:

Principle #8: Energize yourself as a "coach-to-action"

Power Questions:
How can you start to emphasize that you are a "coach-to-action"? When any negative thought about 'selling' comes up, how can you counter that thought with something positive about your coaching the person?

Tom Marcoux

BOOK TWO: INFLUENCE

Who would you like to influence? What would you like to happen as a result of your efforts?

The Merriam-Webster Dictionary defines influence as "the act or power of producing an effect without apparent exertion of force or direct exercise of command."

We see that this process is different from compelling someone to change their mind or do something. To compel is defined as "to drive or urge forcefully or irresistibly . . . to cause to do or occur by overwhelming pressure."

Often when someone tries to compel another person, one thing results: Resistance.

There is a better way: listening and guiding. Influence is not about pushing. Still, you need lots of energy to listen. Along that line, I'll share methods related to the following topics:

1. Use a Secret for When You're Upset But Still Need to

Influence Someone
2. Release Yourself from Emotional Pain and Welcome True Success and Fulfillment
3. Use the Power of Story

Topic #1:
(Book 2: Influence)

Use a Secret for When You're Upset But Still Need to Influence Someone

Would you like to easily persuade people, even if you feel upset? Researchers have found that the more intense our emotions, the more likely that we fall back on childhood conditioning. For some of us, our regression may cause us to yell or to cower. The solution to falling into troublesome behaviors is—in a word—training. What do you accomplish with training? You rehearse better behaviors.

We'll use the O.N. process to develop our capacity and increase our ability to be influential:

O - open to change your physiology
N - nurture yourself with a break

1. Open to change your physiology

It is easier to act yourself into a new way of feeling than to feel yourself into a new way of acting. - Harry Stack Sullivan

If you're having intense emotions and you still need to influence someone, the fastest way to calm down is to change how you use your body.

Why is this important? You can change *how you feel* in how you use your body. Further, you can pay attention to what in your environment triggers you to feel upset.

Your true freedom rests in your choice of how you program yourself. By this I mean, you can take something that triggers you and use a new behavior to keep calm. For example, many of us have heard that deep breathing helps people under stressful conditions. For example, I guide clients to use "Heart Breathing." That's the process of placing your hand on your chest and over your heart. Then you breathe in your nose and out of your mouth. You allow your abdomen to balloon out on an in-breath. Say to yourself an affirmation like, "My heart feels peace." Some of my clients say things like "God relaxes me." Practice Heart Breathing every day and soon just the mere thought of doing heart breathing can lower your stress level.

Here are other ways to use your physiology to your benefit. If you have a tendency to get upset and yell, take control of your own physiology and sit down. Often that simply act can reduce how upset you feel.

For those who may cower under pressure, use the simple act of standing up, which provides two benefits. First, you "take up more space" which is a technique that Lynda Obst, producer of *Sleepless in Seattle*, shared with me. This is part of projecting confidence like you "own the room."

Second, many of us feel a surge of strength when we stand up.

Another detail about Heart Breathing: When you calm down, you have an advantage. You're able to use more of your resources and you can have an expansive perception of a situation. At that time, you'll be able to hear the other person out and find a better way to influence him or her.

2. Nurture yourself with a break

"I'm not a robot," one of my clients said, commenting on

how tired she felt.

Recently, I said to a friend, "The older I get, the more strategic I become about taking breaks." Taking breaks and renewing your personal energy has a big impact on being influential. Let's face it. If you're tired or frustrated, you're ability to positively influence someone may disappear.

Give yourself the gift of a break. You may discover that you only need a few moments to catch your breath. I recall studying for college exams for 12 hours in one day. I studied for 50 minutes and then I'd take a 10-minute walk around the outside of the library building.

I use a method I call "Vary Your Rhythms." I write for a time, then take a walk. Then I write some more. Then I listen to music while assembling a puzzle. A break can be five minutes or 15 minutes, and I return refreshed.

Now, it's your turn. What brief activity might refresh you?

Take care of yourself and raise your energy to influence others with ease.

* * * * * *

To be truly influential, you need to be in a "good space." If you're miserable, you'll radiate that pain, which will repel other people. For this reason, we'll discuss . . .

Topic #2:
(Book 2: Influence)

Release Yourself from Emotional Pain and Welcome True Success and Fulfillment

You ever lose yourself to emotional pain? Would you like to move forward and open the door to new and better?

Imagine showing compassion to yourself. There is a big difference between paralyzing guilt and using regret to change your behavior.

Guilt, for many of us, is a debilitating "spin cycle."

How do you show compassion to yourself? Let's start with the *American Heritage Dictionary's* definition of compassion: "Deep awareness of the suffering of another coupled with the wish to relieve it."

Why is giving yourself compassion important? Answer: You need to guard your energy.

Without compassion, you're tossed on the seas of negative emotion.

But with compassion, you are kind to yourself. You serve as the supportive friend you need.

In addition, if you identify your own suffering—and you take care of yourself—you're less likely to make mistakes that you'll regret.

Here's a helpful process:

The "Before Now . . . Today I am" Method

As an example, we have two people facing the same mistake: letting another day go by without rehearsing for an important presentation.

Catherine tells herself: "Damn! I didn't rehearse again. Stupid! Stupid! I don't have what it takes to keep this job."

On the other hand, Mindy tells herself:

"Before now, I did not rehearse.

But today, I'm calling my friend Chandra and rehearsing the opening two minutes of my speech."

So the pattern is:

"Before now, I did not _____.

But today, I am [taking action]."

Do you see how empowering the *"Before Now . . . Today I am" Method* can be?

You avoid draining your energy with self-recriminations.

See what did not work, and make a new plan.

Here's a question that can help you show compassion to yourself: *Would I treat my best friend this way?*

If not, find a way to encourage yourself and to be kind to yourself.

Eliminate some of your own misery, and you can brighten the world.

You can radiate positive charisma (and you'll be influential).

Good for you and for us all.

* * * * * *

Topic #2:
(Book 2: Influence)
Use the Power of Story

To truly influence someone, you want to sidestep resistance. When someone introduces anything new, we tend to naturally resist. Why? We have two parts of our brain that instantly assess situations for threats.

The emotional brain focuses on preventing loss. If we are presented with something new, the threat may be that we are proved to have been wrong. That's a loss of self-esteem. Many of us will stick to old ideas to avoid feeling wrong. (Remember the resistance to the idea that the earth was not the center of the galaxy and that the sun is.)

The reptile brain focuses on survival. Human beings tend to instantly judge things because they're subconsciously assessing "Will this hurt me?"

Fortunately, we can get around the obstacle of stimulating resistance. A primary way to avoid resistance is to tell a story. I detailed this in my book *Darkest Secrets of Negotiation Masters: How to Protect Yourself, Overcome Intimidation, Get Stronger, and Turn the Power to Good.*

Here are elements of a powerful story:

1. You are a major person in the story.
2. The problem is presented, and it's a tough one.
3. There's a time crunch involved (like a "ticking time bomb").
4. It seems that there is no solution. (This provides suspense and tension.)
5. There is a surprising resolution. (This provides feelings of relief and joy.)

It may not be possible to include all five elements, but it helps to incorporate as many of the elements as possible.

Again, telling a story gives you a special advantage: Often you can avoid generating resistance in the other person. How? We are conditioned from childhood to pay attention to stories, and they give us an experience.

On the other hand, if you make a simple statement, the person automatically goes into "judging mode." The person asks him or herself, "Is that true? Do I believe that?"

Here is a technique I teach my graduate students in my public speaking class: "Don't just state a fact. At least, ask a question."

Asking a question creates a different energy in the room. Just imagine the different audience responses to a statement versus a question:

1) Women live longer than men.
2) Why do women live longer than men?

In addition, statistics can be dry. Instead, telling a story does engage the audience. I'll now share examples of two of my own stories. (I'll present the first couple of sentences of each story.)

- "When I was holding onto the hood of the Classic 50's truck going 60 miles an hour, my finger tips were aching. I wasn't thinking of the cameraman trying to get the shot. I was focused on . . ."
- "When I held the hand of my mother who was awake and undergoing a breast lumpectomy under local anesthesia, I saw in her eyes that the pain . . ."

As you can see, the story puts a listener into the moment. You engage the person's imagination and that gives you the potential to avoid resistance .

Great storytellers can be great influencers.

BOOK THREE: LEVERAGE

What does leverage mean to you? Do you think of it as a means to get something big done? When you want to change the world, it's helpful to become strategic in your actions. That's when you'll employ leverage.

The American Heritage Dictionary of the English Language defines *leverage* as "a. The action of a lever. b. The mechanical advantage of a lever. . . . 2. Positional advantage; power to act effectively . . . . to improve or enhance."

An important distinction is that one can use a lever and exert a small amount of effort and gain a big result.

To exert leverage in a situation is to act strategically and with appropriate care.

Along this line, we'll cover the following topics:

1. Succeed By Erasing the Ceiling
2. Get Beyond Obstacles and Make Your Breakthrough
3. Make Your Impossible Dreams Come True . . . This Year!

4. Use Your Intuition for Success–And Avoid a Misstep

Topic #1
(Book Three: Leverage)
Succeed By Erasing the Ceiling

Do you want big success? Then you'll need to "erase the ceiling." That is, you need to be doing something where you have big potential for growth. For example, one of my friends makes $400 per hour. But that's still a ceiling.

The good news is that you can pursue actions that have an open sky (in this way you increase your leverage). We'll use the W.O.W. process:

W – wonder about new ways to apply your talents
O – open new doors
W – work it and network it

1. Wonder about new ways to apply your talents
Since you're reading these words, you have likely survived and endured some tough times in the past. Who hasn't? Along the way, you've learned things and such knowledge could benefit a novice. For example, I've worked numerous times in a recording studio on movie soundtrack music and songs for a band for which I was lead singer and keyboardist. I know that one can make mistakes in a studio and even "make your ears tired." That means that one could miss details due to fatigue.

So I know to schedule multiple sessions (to come back fresh the next day or next week) and to take appropriate breaks.

With my knowledge about recording in a studio, I could write a short ebook and help others — and have a new source of income.

My point is that you can take what you learned and, perhaps, write a book or lead a workshop and teach others what you learned through hard experience.

Using your hard-earned knowledge and then making a product is about the application of a form of leverage. For example, when one person speaks to a room full of people, the speaker is leveraging her time. She can also make much more income than merely earning an hourly wage. By this I mean, she addresses and serves multiple people at the same time. If she was working for one client and earning an hourly wage she might make $125.00. However, if she is addressing a room of 100 people (ticket price of $39.00) and then selling products ($2500) she makes a total of $6400. Plus these 100 people may be sources of referrals for new business. [These totals are on the low end. After more experience and acclaim, a speaker can earn higher levels of income.]

When I talk about "wonder about new ways to apply your talents," I'm referencing my experience that one can build on past experiences in new job settings. For example, my training as an actor helps me every week when I present to my college students or a business audience.

Now, it's your turn. What are your talents and how might you apply them in a new venue? For example, if you wrote a book, you do the work once and the book sells on Amazon.com while you're sleeping! That's no ceiling.

2. Open new doors

Here's an important distinction of opening new doors: Be sure to go through them! By this I'm suggesting: Merely contemplating new actions or new opportunities does not mean much. I know someone who has talked about doing a software program for fifteen years. But she does not gather a team. She merely enjoys talking about the project. She's also one of the most miserable people I know.

But this is *not* for you.

Use what I call *The Easy Part Start*. Think of a small action you can take so that you try something new. You might take a class; read a few pages of a book each day to become familiar with the new area of interest; or write a paragraph a day of a book or article.

For example, I'm writing a fantasy-thriller titled *Jack AngelSword*. Some time ago, I committed to writing a paragraph each day for 90 days. I learned so much about the characters doing that. How? I noted scraps of dialogue and details of scenes.

It does not matter how slow you go as long as you do not stop.
— *Confucius*

Make a little progress each day.

3. Work it and network it

Nothing works unless you "work it." But there's something to add here. Get expert advice and coaching.

For example, years ago, my father wanted to learn how to ride a unicycle. For weeks, he rode the unicycle next to a wall near his home. He used that wall as his "crutch." I asked, "Dad, how about you hire someone to coach you for 30 minutes?"

He never hired the coach and he never perfected his unicycle-riding. He simply gave up.

But this is *not* for you. Instead, I invite you to "network it," that is reach out to people in your network and ask for referrals to potential experts/coaches who can

- save you time

- save you money
- save you from losing enthusiasm (like my father lost interest in unicycle-riding)

When you want WOW in your life, find ways to do things that have no ceiling.

There is no ceiling to how much a product can earn (as opposed to working for an hourly fee).

Find new ways to apply your talents. You'll leverage your time.

You'll enjoy the adventure and often, surprising, positive results.

For example, a number of my college students are stretching their wings and using kickstarter.com to launch a new creative project.

Here's an example from my former college student Seth Olsen in his words:

"About a year ago, a friend and I realized that people were spending thousands of dollars on the newest and lightest technology and then putting it into large bulky bags. We began to brainstorm. We went through countless designs, many prototypes, a lot of fabric testing and sampling. It was a long process, but it all paid off in the end when I held the very first completed Aurora Laptop Case!

The website www.kickstarter.com was a great venue to reach out to a community of "creatives" for funding. However, before we could even think about that there was so much preparatory work to be done. First we needed to have our implementation plan and budget finalized. We worked with manufacturers, fabric suppliers, photographers, cinematographers and web designers. Our goal was to make $9,500 in 30 days and we thought we had everything in order to do so. Once we began our campaign, we realized just how important marketing really was. We quickly learned that unless we did some intensive marketing, we were not going to reach our goal. Our team was on Facebook, Instagram, Twitter and Tumblr on a daily basis as well as reaching out through email to hundreds of blogs hoping for coverage. This outreach was what made the project possible. The day that Primer (an online magazine) posted an article about us we brought in over $900. Finally during the last few days of our campaign we sent out individual emails and Facebook posts to our backers and enough of them came through which allowed us to reach our goal—and then some!

During the production phase of the process, unforeseen situations came up left and right. We had issues with suppliers, manufacturers and even a mix up when we were trying to receive our funding. It has been a learning process and there is still a lot more to learn. We are constantly rolling with the punches and quickly coming up with new solutions for the everyday challenges. Today, Team Aurora continues to remain excited, optimistic and positive as we move forward with our brand—Aurora by Olson!

Seth Olson
Lead Designer and Co-creator
www.aurorabyolson.com

****

Leverage begins with new ideas and then the willingness to take a step forward.

It's worth it!

* * * * * *

Topic #2
(Book 3: Leverage)
Get Beyond Obstacles and Make Your Breakthrough

Do you long for a breakthrough so that you'll experience big success—and even fulfillment? Two obstacles can stand in your way:
- limiting beliefs
- lack of leverage

1. Shut Down Limiting Beliefs

Consider the lives of Steve Jobs, Oprah Winfrey, Walt Disney, and many top professionals, and you'll see a common thread: They believed that they could make big things happen.

Think like a queen. A queen is not afraid to fail. Failure is another steppingstone to greatness. – Oprah Winfrey

Ordinary thoughts yield ordinary results.
Limiting thoughts demoralize and "de-energize" people.
Here are example of such limiting beliefs:
- "I'll keep getting what I've always gotten."
- "Big lucky breaks are for other people and not me."

I have a word for the above beliefs: Garbage!
There is an old phrase that still holds true: "Garbage in, garbage out."

Instead, build up your stamina with empowering beliefs:
- "I can learn anything I need to."
- "Any day, I can make a breakthrough."
- "I'm actively working with and helping others. Opportunities are naturally flowing to me."

How do you shut down limiting beliefs? Every time a negative thought arises, switch to a positive thought that you have purposely formed to counter it.

Here are examples:

- "They won't like my presentation." ==> "I've rehearsed ten times with ten people. I've learned from all of their feedback. I'm ready."
- "I'm too [young/old] for this job." ==> "I'll demonstrate my value, and I'll find a great match of a job."

Make sure your replacement-thought (positive thought) is reality based. By this I mean, do the rehearsals, get the feedback, and make yourself prepared.

2. Increase Leverage

To put an important idea in a few words: "You've got to be seen doing great work."

Think about leverage. We recognize how a lever can be used to move a boulder. It comes down a small amount of work that makes a big positive result.

To get big things done, you must have the reputation (or personal brand) as a truly competent person who is easy to work with.

For example, top salespeople know that to sell their product to a vice-president in a big corporation, they need a "champion." A champion informs the buyer that you are trustworthy, competent, and caring.

So how do you increase your personal leverage?

You treat other people well. You demonstrate your own competence. You do *not* merely keep your head down and hide. Instead, you keep your supervisor informed of the good work that you're doing.

Do not wait to be "discovered."

Instead, gently let people know what you're

accomplishing and how you're helping others.

I've shared with clients: "If you don't blow your own horn, no one will hear your music."

Imagine someone slamming a hammer upon a rock. When does the rock split? After the one thousandth striking of the hammer. The truth is all 999 other impacts (plus the 1000th impact) were essential.

Keep swinging your hammer.

And let people know your competence, service, and dedication.

* * * * * *

Topic #3
(Book 3: Leverage)
Make Your Impossible Dreams Come True . . . This Year!

What if many of your dreams that appear impossible could actually come true? The truth is that we lack only four elements that can facilitate our making big things happen in our lives. We'll use the G.I.V.E. process:

G – get over denial
I – invest for the long term
V – volunteer for "good risks"
E – encourage leverage

I chose the word GIVE because we need to give our devotion to our dream. We must dedicate ourselves and our best efforts to get big dreams done.

1. Get over denial.
Denial can kill your dream. How? What you do not know and you do not fix can stop your dream cold.

For example, this year will be a breakthrough year for my team. How do I know that? I will do things that I've never done before. About one month ago, we did something we never did before: we completed a graphic novel *Crystal Pegasus* for children, parents, and grandparents to share.

Now, it's my job to . . .
- get coaching from people I've never worked with before
- find new ways to market the graphic novel
- forge new alliances so that a portion of the proceeds benefits children in hospitals
- identify sponsors and connect with them for special printings of the graphic novel so that proceeds go to worthwhile charities.

Do you see how I must do NEW things? That means I must get over any denial that I already have all the people and elements I need at this moment. To get *Crystal Pegasus* to many people, I need new information, new contacts, new coaching, new rehearsals for meetings and phone calls—and more. So I will take positive action in these areas.

Here's another thing we must do: Get over Denial that bad things can happen. The idea is to learn what you need to so that you're strong and savvy.

I have invested my lifetime of study and personal experience into a series of nine books *Darkest Secrets . . . How to Protect Yourself*. Here are the topics of my *Darkest Secrets* book series: persuasion and seduction, negotiation, film directing, acting and self-promotion, spiritual seduction, business communication, personal branding, small business marketing, and making a pitch for Film/TV.

For my readers and my clients, I coach them in ways to become strong and savvy.

Remember, you must be courageous and face any "bad news" and get over denial—then take positive action.

2. Invest for the long term

I know a good writer who does not complete or publish anything—not even by self-publishing. He said, "How do I know if the book will sell? What if I waste my money hiring an editor and a book cover designer?"

I replied, "Richard Carlson told me some years ago that he wrote nine books with varying degrees of success, and that it was his tenth book, *Don't Sweat the Small Stuff*, that was his first best-selling book."

Imagine how, with each completed book, Richard Carlson gained more skill and understanding. In essence, he invested his efforts and learned from each editor in his long-term career.

How might you start today and do small projects to build your career?

3. Volunteer for "good risks"

What is a good risk?

- one that moves your career and dream forward
- one that will leave you better than you started even if something does not go your way

So risking your house on paying for an entrepreneurial project may be a serious problem. You may want to structure a risky venture in a better way.

Many of us have heard about how Steve Jobs poured $30 million into Pixar before there was a true promise of projects on the level of *Toy Story*, *The Incredibles,* and *Finding Nemo*. But even losing $30 million would not have torn Steve Jobs apart.

Not every project my team has done has performed at the level we prefer. But no matter what, our skills have improved, and we have produced better and better work. The previous projects have served as "good risks." And, each project had a budget and plan attached.

4. Encourage leverage

Finally, to make your "impossible" dream come true, you need leverage.

In business, to gain leverage, focus on these 3 *Golden Points of Leverage:*

1) *your network* (your contacts . . . how many people are in your e-subscribers list, connected to you via LinkedIn.com, Twitter, Facebook?)

2) *your special knowledge* (you're an expert; perhaps, you know current marketing trends)

3) *your access to target markets.*

So when you make a presentation in search of the golden "yes" (in business), demonstrate that you have the above 3 *Golden Points of Leverage.*

I invite you to consider the above elements of G.I.V.E. when you consider even for a moment that your dream may be "impossible."

With appropriate coaching, learning, new contacts, new alliances, and new effort, you can make a dream come true.

* * * * * *

Topic #4
(Book 3: Leverage)
Use Your Intuition for Success—And Avoid a Misstep

Have you heard how top successful people follow their intuition? Would you like to follow your heart, but you're afraid of making a big mistake? We'll use the O.W.N. process:
O – open
W – work it through
N – notice

1. Open
Open your thoughts and feelings to the differences between the "Voice of Fear" and the "Voice of Intuition."
- Voice of Fear: contract, hide, play it safe
- Voice of Intuition: expand, experiment, take an appropriate risk.

An old phrase holds: "You can play it safe or play to win."

To make something great happen, you often have to take an appropriate risk. We'll look at the process of taking an appropriate risk with the next step.

2. Work it through
How can you take action based on your intuition and still be okay if things don't go as planned? This is a useful question because listening to your intuition can be more art than science. By this I mean, you might get an intuitive feeling but feel uncomfortable because it does not come with a whole step-by-step plan.

I suggest that you note the intuitive idea and feeling and then pause to think through the various outcomes. As you consider them, also look for a way that you can move forward while minimizing the downside (the trouble that might occur if things don't work out.) [For more information about working well with risks and people, see my book *Darkest Secrets of Charisma: Overcome the Lies about Personal Magnetism, Get People to Feel Your Charisma and Influence Others with Your Words*.]

One way to minimize the downside of a risk is to take a "step-up by step-up approach." Here's an example. Let's say I want to discover what my next book will be. Deciding to do a book is a big decision because producing a book is expensive in terms of time, energy, and investing in topnotch editors, cover designer, and more.

How do you test a title and topic for a book? I try out material with my blog. I take notice when one blog article gains 64 Facebook shares (for example). That gives me a clue that some material strikes a chord with readers.

The next step can be to write a short ebook. If that ebook consistently gains buyers each month, then maybe it's time to expand the work as a paperback book or a Home Study Course.

My point is that I do not take that intuitive thought and immediately "plunge in" with abandon. Such an action might cause a misstep.

Instead, I use the first intuitive thought and feeling as fuel to make a "step-up by step-up" plan. I test things all along the way. That's how I avoid a number of missteps.

One year, a client said, "I'm afraid of climbing higher because I'll have further to fall."

I replied, "We'll work so you bring the safety net up with you."

3. Notice

It's valuable to keep a log of your intuitive ideas, your related actions, and the outcomes. A log helps you observe how your intuition has helped you gain good results. You want to log how the intuitive ideas came to you so that you can make space and welcome more such ideas.

For example, one year, I woke from a dream in which a person whom I had not seen in five years appeared. I took that appearance as an invitation for me to look that person up. During a subsequent phone conversation, the person suggested I contact "Alice." Soon I had an interview with Alice, and then I had a new opportunity.

Going with intuitive ideas can often lead to such new opportunities.

So notice when you get your intuitive thoughts. A number of writers report that they get their best ideas when near water. Some take a walk near a lake; others get a flash of insight while washing the dishes or taking a shower.

To have the full benefit of your intuition, always carry two pens and a notepad—or an audio recorder. Capture the intuitive ideas as they arise.

When you want to rise faster in your career, improve how you relate to your own intuition.

Think of your intuition as another tool in your toolkit. It helps to have access to this resource in addition to any regular thought processes that you use.

Intuition proves so valuable that a number of people have shared their thoughts:

It is through science that we prove, but through intuition that we discover. – Henri Poincare

Trusting our intuition often saves us from disaster.
– Anne Wilson Schaef

Intuition is a spiritual faculty and does not explain, but simply points the way. – Florence Scovel Shinn

Make friends with your intuition.

Remember, leverage occurs when we exert a small effort for a big result.
A good use of intuition can save you time and money.
Here is a useful principle: *If in doubt, leave it out.*
If you have "a bad feeling about something," it's likely good to avoid getting entangled in it.
Numerous individuals say, "I knew this would go wrong. Why didn't I listen to myself?"
Instead, you can pay attention when your intuition speaks to you.
In this way, you can avoid a number of missteps.
And you can improve and enhance your leverage in life.

BOOK FOUR:
EMOTIONAL STRENGTH

When you want to change the world, you need to master your own approach to daily life. Are you making daily progress?

Does every day include something that you want to do? If not, pause right now and imagine that it's possible to turn your life around. What would your better life look like?

To gain the life you truly want, you need perseverance born of emotional strength. For that reason, we will cover the following topics:

1. Don't Let Fear Shut Down Your Creativity!
2. How You Can Start on Your Dream Today.
3. The Big Success Secret: Dig Deep and Open Your Options
4. Move Ahead Successfully Even When You're Criticized
5. How you can Get Strong and Stop Triggers from Running Your Life

Topic #1
(Book 4: Emotional Strength)
Don't Let Fear Shut Down Your Creativity!

One decision can improve your life. It's when you decide to become strong and handle fear. This means a lot to me because I've had to face fear numerous times. Why? Every year I do something for the first time. I'm consistently stretching and growing. My various firsts include: first time directing a feature film, first time being the lead singer/songwriter of a band, first time writing a book, first time teaching a graduate level class and more. I had some fear each time, but I went forward.

How do you effectively face fear and move forward: It comes down to four essential questions:

1) What's your safety net?
When I write a book, I have two editors who push me to better writing. I get support. (And I offer it, too. I recently launched my new Linkedin.com group "Executive Public Speaking and Communication Power!" Consider joining the group.)

2) How can you step past fears about money?
I just started writing my first musical. I've scheduled the work to happen over two years. Why? I'm busy doing other things that are the sources of income. I do not set myself up to have to earn money with the musical. I have the freedom to experiment.

No matter how the musical turns out, I will grow and improve as a writer. It will not interfere with my income-generating work. But it will be a source of fun and creative joy!

So concerns about money will not shut down my creativity. I'm sharing this example to demonstrate that you can find a way to move forward and still take care of your financial needs.

3) How can you do it without needing others to say 'yes'?

When it comes to the musical, I do not have to wait for a theatre troupe to say yes. I can hire singers and record a version of the songs in a recording studio. I can say yes to myself. Maybe one of the songs will work well separately from the musical.

I'm sharing this example of not waiting for a "yes" because fear about others' reactions has paralyzed numerous would-be creators of material. But this is *not* for you. You can find a way to move forward and do a version of whatever you'd like to do.

4) How can you focus on "learning" and overcome fear that "it may not be great"?

Do not let yourself get stuck in having to make anything "great" the first time out. Realize that any art form requires a learning curve.

For example, I know a number of people who have enjoyed *Wicked*, the musical. Some consider it the biggest stage success of composer Stephen Schwartz's career. In October 2010, *Wicked* became the third musical in Broadway history to exceed $500 million in total gross income. And Wicked is Stephen's thirteenth musical. Yes, it's a big hit and it's number 13. He just keeps on getting better!

Don't expect yourself to do it "perfectly" the first time.

We truly learn by doing. When you focus on learning each time you go to the creative well, you always win. Sometimes, you may do a project that does not hit the marketplace at a suitable time. For example, when the film *The Princess Bride* was released, few people saw it at movie theaters. Only later, a core audience found the film when it was released on VHS tape. It became so popular that it's now available on Blu-ray, and it's had a special 25th Anniversary edition. What counts is that you keep exploring and taking appropriate risks.*

This reminds me of the quote:
Don't ask what the world needs. Ask what makes you come alive, and go do it. Because what the world needs is people who have come alive. – Howard Thurman

Keep learning, keep expressing your creativity and you'll find joy in doing the projects. And you'll come alive!

* *Get more encouragement. See my book* Nothing Can Stop You This Year!

* * * * * *

Topic #2
(Book 4: Emotional Strength)
How You Can Start on Your Dream Today

What's your dream? Do want to start a project, a film, a book, something else? The important thing is to "work with what you have." We'll use the G.O. process:

G – get experience

O – organize "criteria for excellence"

1. Get experience

In creating film/video/music projects for over twenty years, I've noticed something: We always want more time and a bigger budget.

Having limits in time and budget means one thing: Important choices must be made.

I've learned that having many creative experiences has given me an instinct for making decisions. Now, *that* is an advantage. I know when to switch gears and when to give people space to explore what they're doing.

So I invite you to start small, right where you're at. *If you're looking for a miracle, start something in motion.*

If you're a novice actor, have a friend use a consumer video camera and film you giving a monologue. If you like it, place it on YouTube.com!

If you're a budding illustrator, pull out a sketchbook and sketch something—anything that captures your attention.

Find your own way to show the world, in a small way, what you can do.

You'll gain experience, and then you'll have a storehouse of insights and, perhaps, even a honed intuition to make your next project better. I know some creative people who took the "short view" and gave up too soon. Picture your lifetime. Just imagine how you'll get better and better at your craft. Sometimes, the breakthrough happens in one year—or five—or ten. However long it takes, enjoy the journey. With so much experience, you'll be ready for your breakthrough when it arrives.

2. Organize "criteria for excellence"

As I mentioned, for each project there are limits of time,

budget, and even the endurance of the participants. Often, "going for perfection" is a moving target—and it may not even be appropriate. What makes a perfect painting?

I once asked a successful author, "How do you know when a book is done?" He said something a bit off color: "How do you know when to urinate?"

Sure, he got some chuckles from the audience. But there was a kernel of truth: The idea was "you just know!"

How do you know what to aim for when you do a project? Pause. Then write down what you choose as "criteria for excellence." Only you know what is most important to be in your project. And at the same time, you choose what to drop or let go.

For example, I'll set a promotional film to be about one minute long. Why? Let's face it: people are really busy. If I say, "How about looking at my film? It's only one minute long," many people will agree.

On the other hand, if I ask them to view something two minutes long, they may resist.

So I've set as one criteria for excellence: "one minute." [See my video at Mayan Ruins and helmet diving under the sea when you type "Jack AngelSword Mayan Ruins" at YouTube.com]

Consider this other facet of setting your own criteria for excellence: You know when it's done. You aim to satisfy yourself. Why? No matter what you do, there's someone out there who will criticize it. And that's fine. It was not for them.

As I share with my graduate students, "At least satisfy yourself. If it moves you, it will move someone else."

Most importantly, start today with what you have. It's really how you grow as a person and as an artist—whether your art is film or living your own full life.

* * * * * *

Topic #3
(Book 4: Emotional Strength)

The Big Success Secret: Dig Deep and Open Your Options

Want more success? Then you need to make better decisions and take better action. You need to dig deep. We'll use the D.I.G. process:

D – drop what's not working
I – intensify your strengths
G – give yourself to new options

1. Drop what's not working

This is an important step. We have truly limited time and resources. Sure, we've heard about having priorities. Just as important is having "drop-ables." Think about it. How do you feel after seeing certain friends or family members? More energized? Drained? I'm not saying to drop a friend completely, but you can just limit the amount of time you interact with a negative person.

In my company, I once gained clear insight by putting various projects on a corkboard. We had 14 projects going simultaneously. In front of that board, I immediately set up a section entitled "for later" and demoted two projects. We were then down to 12 projects. Then I arranged for two other projects to be completed faster. Down to 10 projects.

When you drop some projects, you have more time to "dig deeper" into the projects that are most important. You can devote more time to interacting with team members to ensure things progress with efficiency and high quality.

After dropping some projects, you can truly focus on your

goals. Over the years, I've learned the wisdom in Jim Rohn's comment: "We generally change ourselves for one of two reasons: inspiration or desperation."

Now, I suggest that you combine the energy you get from three types of goals.
- Golden Pull Goals
- Dark Boot Goals
- Green Tranquility Goals.

The real source of strength is to combine all three forms of goals. I'm inviting you to pool the energy of both inspiration and desperation.

Start with a Golden Pull Goal:
A Golden Pull Goal is positive. It pulls you forward. An example is: I want to sing on Broadway.

Add a Dark Boot Goal:
A Dark Boot Goal is negative. It's like a boot hitting you in the rear. It's a goal that is about getting away from something painful. An example is: "I want to quit this job at the fast food restaurant. The pay is so low I cannot keep up with my bills."

Restore Your Energy with a Green Tranquility Goal.
A Green Tranquility Goal is a "being" goal as opposed to a "doing" goal. Here are examples:

- I'll just "be" in a peaceful space by doing a deep breathing meditation for two minutes.

- I'll walk in the park after work for 15 minutes before I return to my boisterous home with two young kids racing around.

- I'll park my car and listen to a soothing tune for five relaxing minutes.

I invite you to dedicate time and effort to become clear on

your true goals and "drop-ables."

2. Intensify your strengths

Beware of "occupational hobbies." An occupational hobby is something that you may like to do, but it's not aligned with your highest strengths. For example, I can use Photoshop to modify photos or work on a book cover. However, my strength truly resides in writing, not in using graphics-related software. I could train with Photoshop for two years and not accomplish what my book cover designer does in fifteen minutes.

When I say "intensify your strengths," I mean:
- devote more time using your true strengths
- eliminate working too much on weaknesses
- improve your skills in your strength-areas

When you work on your strengths, you can rise to the level of world-class. When you work on your weaknesses, you can rise to mediocre. Intensify your strengths.

Yes, I realize that we must devote time to work on certain debilitating weaknesses—like poor listening skills. However, it's important to "strengthen your strength."

3. Give yourself to new options

When I say "give yourself to," I mean to truly devote yourself (and make a full commitment) to what you're working on. Beyond that, talk with appropriate people to see if you're missing something. Maybe you need to look at a problem from new angles.

Recently, I was talking with someone who said, irritably, "I already thought of that! I'm not an idiot." The sad news here is this irritable approach does *not* encourage people to offer him ideas and suggestions, which means he may miss out on a useful idea at some point.

One human being can think of a few ideas. But a group of supportive people can come up with plenty of new options. Such a group can help when encouraged by an open and positive person.

Here's an example of gaining ideas from others: I recently learned from Guy Kawasaki that while fiction sells quite well in ebook form, many readers of business books prefer paperback and hardcover books. With such inspiration from Guy, I have now made my well-received ebook into a paperback entitled *Darkest Secrets of Charisma: Overcome the Lies about Personal Magnetism, Get People to Feel Your Charisma and Influence Others with Your Words*.

When you want a better life than you've ever known, stretch and grow. Make yourself available to new options. Be sure to drop what's not working; intensify strengths and give yourself to new options.

More and better is available to you. This makes life a grand adventure.

* * * * * *

Topic #4
(Book 4: Emotional Strength)

Move Ahead Successfully Even When You're Criticized

Do you want real success and fulfillment? Then, learn to handle criticism in an empowered manner. The crucial detail when facing criticism is to prepare your own personal and empowering questions.

1. Does this person really want good things for me?
2. What are my personal goals, and does this comment strengthen me?

3. Does this comment strengthen my work?
4. Does this comment help me learn and grow?

1. Does this person really want good things for me?

I have an extended family member who has nothing but criticism for me. He's older, and he's never been an entrepreneur, author, educator or feature film director. Those are my areas of expertise. However, this person just wants to make me "wrong." Wait a minute! This is a family member, but his goal is "to be right" and "to put the other person down." It's sad really.

When you consider whether criticism has merit, consider the source. If someone is in your target market, that criticism may be useful. However, if someone is merely guessing and has never entered the field you're working in, assess whether to dismiss such criticism.

Sitting with my negative extended family member feels like resting where good ideas go to die. So I often avoid this person. I have a circle of friends and colleagues who are supportive and still provide me with the constructive feedback that may be hard to hear, but their intention is good things for me. I can trust them.

2. What are my personal goals, and does this comment strengthen me?

What are your real goals? Do you want to be famous? Do you want to do good artistic work? Do you want to make lots of money? Do you deeply long to express your creativity?

All of the above have different elements attached to them.

It's important for you to be honest with yourself. What do you really want?

The truth is that I want to serve my readers, audiences,

graduate students, and clients. So I'm willing to hear tough feedback and learn about areas to improve for my projects. For each book I write, I have at least two editors. They can be really tough, and they push me to write in better ways. That's what I really want. I do not want to be coddled.

So even if my editors might occasionally clothe a comment with sarcasm, I still know that their comments actually strengthen me. After writing 19 books, I'm a better writer today.

Also, pause and get access to your own intuition. Often, some people are so quick to judge and say, "That won't work." How do they know? And imagine this: If your intuition is correct and you follow your heart—and you succeed—what will they say? They'll merely shrug and mildly reply, "Oh, I guess I was wrong on that one."

Do not leave your fate to someone else. Answer your own heart's call.

3. Does this comment strengthen my work?

This is where the real work takes place. A tough comment like "I think that totally fails to engage your target market" may be the best reality check that you need. For example, with a video related to my science fiction franchise *TimePulse*, my team hit a wall. We needed a paragraph to bridge two sections of the video. I had four people tell me that the paragraph we chose missed the mark. Okay. Back to the drawing board. Eventually, we came up with a solution. With a new approach, we found an appropriate quote to bridge the sections. We realized that our critics had been right, and their comments led to changes that made our video better and stronger. [See our one-minute video of science fiction and action, *TimePulse from Tom Marcoux* on YouTube.com]

4. Does this comment help me learn and grow?

My team members know that I can calmly listen to any comment that points out flaws in a draft of a project. I'll often ask follow-up questions. Why? I'm focused on learning and growing as an artist in the various fields I participate in: speaking, writing, filmmaking, and art direction of graphic novels.

My point is that a truly creative person must develop a "thick skin" and also run criticism through a filter. Some critical comments have nothing to do with your goals. Let them flow past you like leaves on a stream of water.

Other comments which are given to support you and which strengthen your work may raise your work to world-class level. It's an adventure that is actually worth the pain and effort. It's a road that includes surprising, happy moments.

* * * * * *

Topic #5
(Book 4: Emotional Strength)
How to Have a Good Day Every Day

Do you want to experience joy and success each day? Have you heard that you need to live in the present and not just for a fabled future? We'll use the S.E.E. process:

S – serve to brighten someone's day
E – express your creativity and find joy in it
E – expand for a better tomorrow

1. Serve to brighten someone's day

For many of us, if we say a kind word and a friend smiles in response, we feel better.

Happiness often sneaks in through a door you didn't know you left open. – John Barrymore

By expressing kindness, you leave open multiple doors.

By the way, be kind to yourself, too. If you're compassionate to yourself, you'll have the energy to be patient and kind to others. This is one of the principles of increasing your emotional strength.

2. Express your creativity and find joy in it

Many of us find joy in doing something creative. Perhaps you like to do a hobby: knitting, jogging, or painting. People also express creativity in finding ways to be supportive to a friend or family member.

Expressing creativity is simply a fun and fulfilling way to be alive.

3. Expand for a better tomorrow

Feeling hopeful about your next day, next week, and next few years feels good. How do you create such hopeful feelings? You set a plan and work your plan on a daily basis. I know a teacher who feels good about how she is kind to the children in her care. Each night she writes a few pages of her first novel. She hopes to make novel writing the new chapter of her life. Even if she continues as a teacher and writes novels on the side, she is still "expanding for a better tomorrow." Her future is not limited to only her present job activities.

Maybe she might become a fiction editor. Many of us find that each new chapter of life builds on the previous ones.

And we get delightful surprises. Someone begins as a singer at church, sings in a band and has some success, and later finds fulfillment as a singing teacher. We do not know what exactly lies ahead. A helpful principle (and affirmation) is: "I'll serve wherever I am."

Often I have heard:
- You better enjoy today. You might not have tomorrow.
- You need to live in the present.

I wondered how to do that well.

Now, we can *see* our way clear. With the S.E.E. process, I'm not denying that we can have things go wrong at times. In fact, I wrote this article while experiencing some digestive tract pain. So I learned how to be at peace while feeling some discomfort. I did not feel bad the entire day. Instead, I call the difficult times: "bumpy moments." I do not expect to be free of all problems in order to have a good day. I have good days with occasional "bumpy moments."

Don't judge each day by the harvest you reap but by the seeds that you plant. – Robert Louis Stevenson

Let's enjoy the good moments given in each day.
Today is your day. Enjoy.

* * * * * *

Topic #6
(Book 4: Emotional Strength)

How You Can Get Strong and Stop Triggers from Running Your Life

"Why can't you just back me up on this?!" Jonathan yelled, and his girlfriend Nancy winced. He didn't know that hearing one detail (about Nancy's father) would trigger such a big reaction in him. At Nancy's words, a visceral childhood memory arose for Jonathan, and suddenly cortisol dumped in his blood stream and his heart raced, and he just reacted.

For many people who read self-help books or attend therapy, progress toward getting better can seem slow. They must learn how to deal with triggers that cause automatic and reflexive reactions. It's time for them to H.E.A.L.:

H – hear the trigger
E – enlighten
A – act to replace
L – leap back

1. Hear the trigger

You can't heal what you don't notice. Remember a time when someone said, "Hear him out." Pause. Pay attention. Notice if you're upset. Ask yourself:

- What's going on here?
- Am I upset for the reason I think—or is there something else going on?
- What could that be?
- Has something happened now that has stimulated my brain and body to react? Is the reaction really about something from my past?

Hear yourself. Notice what trigger (in your daily life) knocks you back in time to reactions from your younger/weaker self. Without awareness or reflection, we may find ourselves living in a reactive way to patterns from our past.

2. Enlighten

Shine light into dark corners, and they lose their power.

When you answer the above questions, you start to shine light on dark corners. Insight alone is *not* enough. But we need to start with questions. Then, we find some answers and prepare for appropriate action.

3. Act to replace

Now that you know you have a trigger that gets you to jump back into a past-related feeling, you have a choice. You can let yourself fall back into mere reaction, or you can choose to instill an Empowered Response. In other words, you can create an Empowering Trigger Sequence (ETS). What kind of sequence? It's a behavior-sequence that functions like this:

- Something happens [the Trigger]
- You notice how you feel
- You put your reaction "on pause"
- You use a preset Empowered Response
- You feel better

Several years ago, I would run with my father. After each run, we'd stop at a convenience store and get an ice cream cone.

Whoa! Stop!

That's like calories out (run) and put them right back in (ice cream cone).

What would be an Empowered Response? Drink some water and have an orange.

You see, the water and orange replace the ice cream cone.

If you take out a bad habit, you have a hole in your behaviors. Fill that void by setting up an Empowered Response.

In this way, you "act to replace" a reaction with an

Empowered Response.

4. Leap back

Do you want to remain a "triggered person"? Or do you want to be strong and proactive? To do this, learn to "leap back." That is, learn to step back and observe your behavior. Does a particular behavior help you live well: healthy, whole, and enjoying abundance? If not, get to work and change it.

One part of "leaping back" may be to install a Pattern-Interrupt. For example, one of my clients sits on the floor during a heated argument with a loved one. Sitting down helps my client to calm down. Find similar behaviors that work for you.

If you are using self-help books as part of your process, remember that reading them is *not* enough. Be sure to actually do the exercises in the book.

If you are having trouble creating effective change on your own, seek assistance from a counselor.

Your real power is in the choices you make of your own programming.

You'll be glad you took action to work on your triggers and behavior-sequences.

And I'm cheering for you.

* * * * * * *

Building Emotional Strength is marked by making good decisions. As I've mentioned earlier, it is valuable to make a Cool Decision so that you have good behavior patterns in place during a stressful or Hot Event. Now, I'll share a guest article by author Chip Conley.

Distinguishing Between a Calling and Workaholism
by Chip Conley

Are you a workaholic or a "work-a-frolic"? The term "workaholism" is now forty years old, but the average American works two hundred more hours per year today than they did when this word was first coined. Spend a day and maybe an evening watching someone intensely dedicated to their work and it's hard to distinguish between whether the person is exhibiting the symptoms of workaholism or whether they're just living their calling.

In order to distinguish the difference, you can't just rely on external appearances. Instead, you must look within the person (or yourself). When someone is living their calling, they've tapped into some deeper reservoir in themselves or in the collective consciousness in such a way that their work energizes their soul as opposed to depleting them. This person is living Khalil Gibran's quote "Work is love made visible." It's almost like "invisible hands" are directing you and you can exhibit many of the qualities of self-actualization and being "in the flow": losing a consciousness of the self, losing track of time, having moments of inspiration and insight throughout the day, and feeling a combination of passion and, most importantly, peace of mind. When you are at one with your calling, you have developed a certain intimacy with who you are and what your purpose is on this planet.

A workaholic prefers not to experience intimacy ("in to me see") as typically – as with most addictions – they are using their work as a means of distraction. Quite often, we get intoxicated with something that alters our mood (including work), partly because we feel compelled to run away from emotions or fears that prey upon us. Scratch the emotional surface of any addict, and underneath you'll find some common emotions: a feeling of unworthiness, a feeling of being unlovable or shame, and a belief that success can become the magic wand that will turn their life around. Workaholism equals "What are you running from?" divided by "What are you living for?" Those that have tamed their workaholic tendencies have taken Henry David Thoreau's quote to heart: "the cost of something is measured by how much life you have to give for it." Reacquainting oneself with what they're living for and calculating the "opportunity cost" of the addiction is a profound way to help a workaholic wake up to what this addiction is costing them.

Here's a quick test that can help distinguish between one who is living a calling versus one who is addicted to their work. Look at the following eight statements and pick the four that best describe your relationship with your work.

1. I often feel like the work I'm doing is coming from some greater source than just me. It's like I'm channeling this energy or talent, and I'm amazed by its power.

2. If I'm not working, I still prefer being busy as I find just sitting and doing nothing to be a waste of time and it makes me a little uncomfortable.

3. I love my work. There's nothing else in my life that gives me nearly as much self-esteem as doing my job well.

4. While I am passionate about what I do, when I am engaged in activities with others or on vacation, I'm able to give all my attention to that without thinking about my work.

5. I have a pretty distinct end goal for my work. I believe that having a clear, defined goal will more likely help me be successful. And, with that success will come more professional respect and happiness.

6. Occasionally, I feel sort of compulsive about my work, especially during times when other things in my life aren't going all that well. For me, work helps create order in my life and that makes me feel better.

7. It seems like the deeper I get into my work, the less ego I have about the work. I sort of lose myself and almost feel like I'm trying to recover my sense of the miraculous about life.

8. There's no way I could do anything else but what I'm doing. If I were doing the average job, I probably wouldn't be able to apply myself very well at it and I'm sure I wouldn't dedicate nearly as many hours.

If you (or someone in your life) chose answers 1, 4, 7, and 8, you scored a perfect 100% for having a calling. The other four answers skew more toward someone who may have a workaholic tendency in their work. While this test isn't scientific, it just gives you a sense of some of the causal factors for a calling versus workaholism.

In my life, I've experienced my work in both of these ways. I know that when I attached my sense of identity a little too closely to my work that I might be distracting myself from feelings of unworthiness. It wasn't the number of hours I worked or how bloodshot my eyes were that defined the difference. It was something internal.

In the early days of my first hotel, The Phoenix, friends would ask me, "How's life, Chip?" I would respond, "The Phoenix is doing well," even when – as a 26 year old entrepreneur – I was pretty nervous my company might not make it. One day a friend who wasn't satisfied with my answer put her hand on my heart and said softly, "Chip, I didn't ask you how your business is doing. I want to know how you're feeling." For most addicts, friends and family see our predicament before we can acknowledge it.

Chip Conley

Hotel guru. Armchair psychologist. Traveling philosopher. Author. Speaker. Teacher. Student. Chip Conley has lived out more than one calling in his lifetime. Founder and former CEO of Joie de Vivre (JDV), Chip has led the development, creation, and management of more boutique hotels than anyone else in the world. Starting JDV at age 26, his mission was to "create joy" by building a company that USA Today called "the most delightfully schizophrenic collection of hotels in America." During his 24 years as CEO, JDV grew to become the second largest boutique hotel company in America.

Chip shares his unique prescription for success in *PEAK: How Great Companies Get Their Mojo from Maslow*, based on noted psychologist Abraham Maslow's iconic Hierarchy of Needs. The *New York Times* bestseller, *EMOTIONAL EQUATIONS: Simple Truths for Creating Happiness + Success*, is Chip's latest book where he takes us from emotional intelligence to emotional fluency – placing meaning at the top of the balance sheet. His previous books include *The Rebel Rules: Daring to be Yourself in Business*, and *Marketing That Matters: 10 Practices to Profit Your Business and Change the World*. Chip presents his theories on transformation and meaning – in business and life – to audiences around the world and he's been a featured speaker at TED.

The San Francisco Business Times named Chip the Most

Innovative CEO. Chip received his BA and MBA from Stanford University and holds an Honorary Doctorate in Psychology from Saybrook University, where he is the 2012/2013 Scholar- Practitioner in residence. He is now on the Boards of the Burning Man Project, the Esalen Institute, and Youth Speaks. Chip's latest calling is traveling the globe – speaking about transformative business practices and seeking out the world's best festivals. He's on a mission to cultivate more cultural curiosity by sharing the "collective effervescence" found in the festival experience.

www.ChipConley.com

BOOK FIVE:
EFFECTIVE SELLING IS
"COACHING-TO-ACTION"

When you want to change the world, you will likely need to "enroll people in your vision." That is, you'll need to encourage them to do something: listen further, sign up for a class, buy a product, or, perhaps, change their pattern of behaviors. An old phrase is: "People like to buy, but they don't like to be sold." This means that many people feel that "being sold" is being manipulated into making a purchase. So let's drop the old view of selling. Instead, let's use a different paradigm of "coaching to action."

(At this point, I'll be using some sales terms. An old phrase is "Nothing happens until somebody sells something." Here we'll hold to the idea of "Nothing happens until somebody 'coaches someone to action.'")

You'll need the skills of an effective coach-to-action. We'll use the C.O.A.C.H. process:

C - create customer delight
O - open real rapport
A - alleviate pain

C - concentrate on "leverage through champions"
H - honor Effort-Goals and Result-Goals

1. Create Customer Delight

What's the most important thing that top salespeople do? They create customers who are more than satisfied. They create customers who are delighted. Delighted customers are the source of valuable leads—which reduce sales cycles. In a few words, **customer delight is something extra and surprising.**

When I interviewed Marty Rodriguez (the #1 real estate agent for Century 21), she said, "My business is now completely by referral." Now that is a way to double your sales in half the time!

Marty pointed out that when she began, she went beyond the call of duty in her service to customers. Her family members helped first-time owners prepare their homes for selling by cleaning windows and more. Marty told me, "People like to hang around our office, and they bring their friends."

When you create customer delight as Marty has done, you create situations in which people enjoy referring business to you.

Another part of creating customer delight is customer satisfaction. Customer satisfaction is achieved when the product arrives on time, for the agreed price—and it functions as advertised. Any vendor can do that. However, customer delight is providing something extra and surprising. When I talked with Mariam Chen, CEO of Chen and McKlinley, the 18th largest woman-owned company in the San Francisco Bay Area, she agreed with my concept of customer delight. She said, "With customer delight, clients are not just satisfied. They are trusting you. My clients feel comfortable in calling me and saying, 'Mariam, please help me with this.'"

7 Secrets to Convert Prospects to Customers via Customer Delight

The Customer Delight Factor is "Do something extra and surprising."

Secret #1: Express appreciation for the person upon your first contact.

Dottie Walters, the late best-selling co-author of *Speak and Grow Rich* and president of Walters International Speakers Bureau, expressed appreciation for everyone she met. She once said, "When I meet someone, whether I know them or not, I say, 'You know, what I like about you…' And I find something."

Here are some of Dottie's examples:
"What I like about you is your voice."
"What I like about you is that you listen."
"What I like about you is that you don't get flustered. During that crisis just a moment ago you just held your calm."

Secret #2: Write a note of congratulations.

Dottie Walters said, "I write to many people. One hundred letters a day. I notice in a trade paper an article, and I write and congratulate the person. And I insert our materials. Often, the person becomes our loyal client." Dottie described a time when she sent a note of congratulations to a particular man who had been noted in a major publication. He responded, "You know, you were the only one who noticed."

Secret #3: Write or say "thank you."

Dottie said, "I think of people to say 'thank you' to. Every day, you need to think 'what have I done to advance my career today?' Do something even if it's only writing 20 thank-you letters." I would suggest sending a thank you card by standard mail (not email); you will stand out.

Secret #4: Offer information.

Marty Rodriguez, the #1 real estate agent in the world for Century 21, offers information especially for first-time sellers of their family home. She will counsel them and say, "You've got to clean the house. You've got to wash the windows." She goes a step further by making them aware of available resources: "We refer them to service people we know. [And we] try to simplify the process for them."

Secret #5: Offer a helpful process.

Marty Rodriguez also offers a process for people trying to reduce their taxes. She explains that it is "an analysis for reducing property taxes. [The prospects] can do it themselves with our help. It's a free service we offer, that some [other real estate professionals] don't bother with."

Another example of offering a helpful process comes from Kathy Aleman, a Senior Coordinator with Shaklee, an international firm that provides nutritional supplements and other products. She offers a free health evaluation form that helps prospects target their health needs. When a prospect fills out the form, it provides information that Kathy uses in her presentation to that person.

Secret #6: Offer something extra.

As I mentioned earlier, Marty Rodriguez now has a

complete referral business. She laid the foundation for that achievement by offering extra services early in her career. She says, "When we just started, my husband did a lot to help people prepare their homes for sale—scraping the windows or cleaning up the property—you name it."

Marty emphasizes one situation: "We closed the deal, and then the client's house was vandalized. She was crying. I said, 'Ed, go over there. Fix it. Make her happy'." After Marty's husband assisted in the repairs, the client became very loyal and helpful to Marty. "A terrible situation was turned into a great one," Marty noted.

Marty goes out of her way to help people, including those who do not speak English. Often, people who do not understand English will receive mailings from scammers that look official but aren't. Marty helps them avoid costly mistakes. She tells them, "Don't mail money in. Let me see it, and I'll tell you if it's legitimate or not." Marty summed up her approach: "One time my husband asked, 'Why do you do these things? You don't have to do these things.' I said, 'That's what makes me different.'"

Secret #7: Put yourself on a vigorous schedule to create customer delight

You must set up a schedule and track your progress in creating customer delight. You do this by following a principle that I share with my coaching clients: *Keep Score and Achieve More.*

I suggest that you keep a log of the thank-you cards and notes of congratulations you send. You can call it your Daily Tracking Plan. The details you record on your log will help create customer delight. When prospects are delighted, more of them will convert to clients.

Once you have your log in place and start using it

regularly, you need to stretch and do more than the average person to gain new business.

You can move beyond what you consider your current limits. Here's an example of stretching beyond perceived limits. At one point, I wanted to learn how notables in the beauty industry sell to salon owners. I went backstage (at a convention) and interviewed Katherine Altieri, a top person in the beauty industry. She described how she went beyond perceived limits. She created dynamic shows to energize hair stylists and salon owners. These shows were a cross between a top pop-singer and *Edward Scissorhands*. Katherine said, "I get an entire show together, wardrobe and everything [dancing and more], within one month. Most people would take six months to a year to put together our kind of show. A lot is involved, but I work better under stress."

Why does Katherine push herself like this? She's making the best possible show which excites the salon owners. A great show creates a powerful impression that leads to credibility and more sales.

To help you focus on valuable actions, I devised a form to help you use these *7 Secrets to Convert Prospect to Customers.*

Here is an example of how such a form would look when filled out:

7 Secrets to Convert Prospects to Customers – Plan (sample – filled out)

Today's date: 5-18-xx
Prospect: Sarah Neuperson
Company: Sombodio, Inc
Phone#: 415-555-1243

Secret #1: Express appreciation for the person upon your first contact.
Tell her, "Sarah, you know what I like about you? You always find creative solutions." . . . Due Date May 23rd

Secret #2: Write a note of congratulations.
Congratulate her on her promotion to vice-president . . . Due Date May 27th

Secret #3: Write or say "thank you."
Send her a postcard thanking her for her time on the phone . . . Due Date May 24th

Secret #4: Offer information.
Email her the article about time-saving strategies (since she mentioned her intense schedule) . . . Due Date May 28th

Secret #5: Offer a helpful process
Offer her a free productivity assessment . . . Due Date May 29th

Secret #6: Offer something extra.
Provide a three-month follow-up process . . . Due Date June 1st

Secret #7: Put yourself on a vigorous schedule to create Customer Delight.

(Customer Delight results from something that is extra and surprising.)

Do today: Meet her at networking event

Plan for this week of May 18th:

Plan for this month of May 2xxx:

Meet with her for free Productivity Assessment

Plan for this year of 2xxx:

Complete 3 phases of training with her and her department

* * *

The Essence of Customer Delight and Your Fresh Approach

When you're active in the process of customer delight, you can feel good about yourself because you're bringing more good into the world. You're making someone's day better and, perhaps, easier.

The experience of customer delight for the buyer is a positive state of being.

When you want to speed up your sales, learn to "Change Your Buyer's State."

When I say "state," I mean state of being. Does your buyer feel comfortable? Empowered? Confident? You can change the buyer's state by simply asking a few effective questions.

Here's an example:

Sarah (salesperson): "What was the last big purchase you made?"

Mark (prospective buyer): "My house."

Sarah: "I'm curious. When you absolutely knew that that house was for you—that it was the one—what happened?"

As Sarah hoped, Mark's entire demeanor changed. A smile flowed onto his face, and his posture became straighter. By changing her prospect's state, Sarah made him feel better—and increased her odds of creating a sale.

I've seen this happen before my eyes, and it can happen for you, too.

Here's the secret: you're linking this positive emotion to your product or service. If you can create this positive state within the buyer while he's holding your product or brochure, all the better.

For some readers, the above process may sound like a mechanical technique. But it doesn't have to be if you begin with a positive intention to help people—and, in particular, to help this person in front of you. Then this sales technique is merely a part of your process. If you know that your product is not a match, then ask for a referral. Avoid pushing or "convincing" the person.

Points to Remember:

Principle #1: Create Customer Delight

Your Action Steps:

Write up a plan for each potential customer you meet. Include:

Secret #1: Express appreciation for the person upon your first contact.

Secret #2: Write a note of congratulations.

Secret #3: Write or say "thank you."

Secret #4: Offer information.

Secret #5: Offer a helpful process.

Secret #6: Offer something extra.

Secret #7: Put yourself on a vigorous schedule to create customer delight.

(Customer delight results from something that is extra and surprising.)

* * * * * *

2. Open Real Rapport

When coaching clients in persuasion skills, I emphasize, "When you're listening, you're creating rapport."

At Dictionary.com, *rapport* is defined as "1) relation characterized by harmony, conformity, accord, or affinity and 2) confidence of a subject in the operator (as in hypnotism, psychotherapy, or mental testing) with willingness to cooperate."

To gain rapport, start by asking a gentle question.

Let's say you're at a networking event.

You can ask: "Hi, I'm [your name], and you are?"

Then ask another gentle question, something like:

"Oh, how do you know Susan Smith?"

"Have you been to many of these events?"

"Which speaker at this conference really gave you information you can use?"

Be sure to listen closely.

Here are steps for listening closely:
- Turn your body squarely toward the person.
- Lean in a bit.
- Make sounds like "mm-hmm" to show that you're listening.
- When appropriate, repeat some of their words to assure them that you have been listening. For example, you might

say, "What I heard you to say is Part X-7 is most important to you. Do I have that about right?"

From Improvisational Theater use "Yes and"
When you talk with someone, you're actually engaging in an improvisation. Consider using an improvisational theatre technique. This particular technique is called "Yes and."

In improvisational theater, your scene partner may say, "I heard that your father just arrived on the shuttle from Neptune."

You reply, "Yes. And the shuttle arrived late. An asteroid took out its aft engine and—"

In everyday life, you create rapport by going along with the other person's comments (if appropriate).

Here is an example:

Joseph: "Man, it's stupid to have the XLZ process tacked onto the 1-2-3 methodology."

Mark: "That's sounds frustrating." [This is like saying, "Yes. You're right."]

Joseph: "You bet it is. And it gets worse . . ."

For creating rapport, realize that people tend to like people who are similar to them. So by going along with the person's comment and doing "Yes and," you're creating that connection.

Points to Remember:

Principle #2: Open Real Rapport

Your Action Step:
Ask gentle questions. Then listen closely.

Here are steps for listening closely:
- Turn your body squarely toward the person.
- Lean in a bit.
- Make sounds like "mm-hmm" to show that you're listening.
- When appropriate, repeat some of their words to assure them that you have been listening.

* * * * * *

3. Alleviate pain

Researchers notice that people will do more to avoid pain than to gain pleasure. So in order to double your sales in half the time, you need to gently help the buyer feel the pain of not getting your product or service.

Wait a minute! Let's look closely at a core principle of this book: We drop "convincing" and enjoy persuading people. Remember my point I shared early on, that persuading (the way we're talking about it) is a process in which you begin with the buyer's well-being in mind. In this way, you serve the person, and you feel good about your daily activities. Convincing is pushing, manipulating, and playing a game. On the other hand, persuading is serving, guiding, and supporting. This is big difference. When you persuade a person to accept an appropriate product or service for his or her well-being, you alleviate their pain.

Let's look closely at "gently help the buyer feel the pain . . ." One interviewer asked me, "You want them to feel miserable? That's not very nice."

I replied, "You're there to alleviate pain. Think of it: every great product or service eliminates pain on some level. For example, I dislike and feel bad about the waste of my time. If I use a voice recognition device that helps me write a book more efficiently, the device has eliminated my pain about having so much to do and maybe losing time that I could put into doing something else."

I continued, "The truth is that the buyers are already feeling pain. Something brought them to you. Often, a potential buyer is so distracted that the pain (or problem) exists only on a subconscious level. What you do, as the effective salesperson [coach-to-action], is to help bring the pain to light—in a gentle way."

You can ask a question like:

- "What obstacles stand between where you are now and ideally where you want to be with _____? And how does that affect you personally?"

The above questions assist you in helping the buyer identify his or her personal concerns. You notice the phrase "how does that affect you personally." Why is this important? Often people are simply more focused on their personal concerns and not the elements that may affect the company where they're employed.

Once you've helped the buyer identify personal concerns, give the buyer an experience of how your product alleviates such pain. How? One powerful method is to identify and rehearse a number of stories relating how previous clients have had excellent results. Then you share an appropriate story with the buyer.

What to Do About Alleviating a Different Type of Pain: "Buyer's Remorse"

Buyer's remorse occurs when a buyer regrets making a buying decision. It hurts the buyer, and, of course, it hurts the salesperson because the deal has evaporated. Once someone experiences buyer's remorse, he can become wary of making future purchases. Even if a buyer has not experienced it himself, his influencers may have, and their objections may affect his decision making.

So how do you counter this situation? You "Embed the Antidote" to the potential poison that may taint your sale. You get the buyer into an empowered state. You do this by asking a useful question and then continuing the process as illustrated below:

Joe (salesperson): "You can just see the fireplace with the glowing fire, right? You can feel the warmth of the fire. Good. You're sitting back. Relaxing. Now, at some point, you might find that when you talk with your wife, she might bring up a concern. What might that be?"

Stephen (buyer): "She'll say the house costs too much."

Joe: "And you'll say, 'I hear you about that important concern.' Then you'll pull out this Assessment Sheet that shows how paying the mortgage on the new house actually is lower than your current renting costs. What would you say at that time?"

Stephen: "I'd say, 'You can see it all right here on this page. I've gone over the numbers carefully. You can check my math, too.'"

A salesperson helps the buyer out by assisting the buyer to come up with his own good answers to his wife's concern.

Then the salesperson checks if this is working by asking a question like: "So the Assessment Sheet and checking the math would answer your wife's concern?"

I call the above process "Embedding the Antidote." Some trainers call this process "Future Pacing" because you make the buyer strong and able to handle a loved one's future objections.

Once again, I want to make the metaphor of Embedding the Antidote clear:

When the buyer is with you, the buyer is feeling good, confident about his or her decision.

But you need to make your buyer strong so that when she or he goes into the cold, cruel world, the buyer is armed with good answers. If the buyer's spouse, accountant, or friend puts poison into your buyer's mind, you have already protected the sale because you have already Embedded the Antidote.

Points to Remember:

Principle #3: Alleviate Pain

Your Action Steps:
Connect with the prospective customer's pain. Use questions like:

"What obstacles stand between where you are now and ideally where you want to be with _____? And how does that affect you personally?"

Then speak of your product or service in terms of how it relieves the prospect's pain.

* * * * * *

4. Concentrate on "Leverage through champions"

Leverage is doing the least effort for the most results. In sales, professionals often remark, "It's a numbers game. You need to see a lot of people."

Top salespeople know that they can fine-tune their sales efforts by finding a "champion." A champion is someone in the company that you're targeting who can help you make the sale.

Make a Distinct, Positive Impression

When I interviewed Barry J. Farber (best-selling author of *Diamonds In the Rough*), he told me the story of how he sold 50,000 copies of his book to an organization. After repeated contacts with 'Susan,' Barry was told that the decision-making committee had rejected the book. Barry said that he was willing to do anything—even travel across the country and paint Susan's new house—in order to get his book order accepted. Two days later, Susan received a paint brush wrapped in cellophane and paint-color brochures. Barry's note read, "I'm ready to paint your house. I'm never giving up." Weeks later, Barry heard that his book was re-evaluated and that he had closed the sale. By the way, Barry's paint brush was mounted on Susan's office wall!

The way you gain a champion is to *Focus on Helping People:*

Here are two benefits: a) you feel good about yourself during the sales process and b) you gain more sales as you act as a trusted advisor.

Magic Networking Words:

Here are examples:
"How can I help you with what you're doing?"
"How can I help make your job a little bit easier?"
"How can I be supportive with what you're doing?"

The Magic Formula for a Complete Referral Business

Since I've mentioned Marty Rodriguez earlier, I'll share what I learned from her and have refined as a Magic Formula:
- Offer a process to help your prospect.
- Offer extras.
- Be very accessible.

A Proven Secret to Help People via Voicemail

The secret is to respond extremely quickly to a voicemail even if you do not have the answer. I learned this from Al Gilbert, a top sales manager in corporate travel (closing $8 million dollar deals). Al points out these details:

"The thing we all fear is being ignored...I respond to voicemail as soon as possible."

"A voicemail is a plea for help out there in the wilderness."

"People buy on emotion, and they validate on fact. The emotion they respond to is the people who listen to them fastest."

Al Gilbert has even responded by telephone while on an airplane, saying, "I don't have the answer because I'm on my way into Chicago. As soon as I get there, I'll look it up for you."

Use the *How I Can Help Plan* to Ensure that You Take Great Action

Using the following form, the "How I Can Help Plan," will help you gain the leverage of having a "champion" assist you towards getting a sale in a company.

This form helps you target how you can *help* the champion, prospect, or client.

It does not take much for someone to be predisposed to

being your champion. For example, about twenty years ago, I met someone at a networking event. I mentioned that I was a film director. She said that she saw an article about director Jodie Foster. Soon she sent me the article, and I chose her company to call first when I was hiring temporary employees. Why? By sending me the article, she proved that she was trustworthy.

Here is the sample form as filled out.

How I Can Help Plan (sample form – filled out)
Customer/Prospect Name *Susan Sombodio*
Company *Sombodio, Inc.*
Position *President*
Phone Number *415-555-1243*
Web Site URL *www.sombodiostuff.com*
Benefits You Will Provide for Customer
   Increase productivity
Business Field *Custom Jewelry*
How can I help/Deadline: *Provide an article about trends in her industry   May 18th*
How can I make the prospect's job a bit easier?
   Increase productivity
How can I help/Deadline: *Provide article about our training that was in Productivity Magazine May 20th*
Hobby *Windsurfing*
How can I help/Deadline: *Provide article from Windsurfing Magazine May 25th*
Family: significant other's interest *Husband likes karate*
How can I help/Deadline: *Provide article about karate May 30th*
Daughter's interest *Brittney BigStar*
How can I help/Deadline: *Have a source for hard-to-get tickets June 4th*

Son's interest *N/A*
Client's Career Goals *76% market share*
How can I help/Deadline: *Provide Training Phase 1,2,3 June 4th*
College? (other experiences) *Smaldand City College*
How can I help/Deadline: *Reunion is September 8th*
Favorite sports team *N/A*
Favorite entertainment activity *Orchestra performance*
How can I help/Deadline: *Send catalog of local events May 18th*
Favorite personal exercise *Stationary bicycle*
How can I help/Deadline: *Article about book stand for reading books while on bicycle May 18th*

* * * **End of Above Form** * * *

Points to Remember:

Principle #4: Concentrate on "Leverage Through Champions"

Your Action Step:
For each prospective client, start filling out a copy of the *How I Can Help Plan*.

Discover how you can be helpful to the person. (My principle of networking is: Help them first.)

* * * * * *

5. Honor Effort-Goals and Result-Goals

Effort-Goals always make you feel good because they are what you can control. *Result-Goals* are the accomplishments you are working to achieve. The difficulty is that Result-

Goals are heavily influenced by other people's action or inaction.

Here is an example of the difference between the forms of goals. An Effort-Goal could be to make five marketing calls daily. A Result-Goal is to gain an extra customer weekly. Remember you can always feel proud yourself when you complete your Effort-Goals.

Effort-Goals grow naturally from your values, that is, what is most important to you. To target your values, I invite you to answer these following questions in your personal journal. (Since Effort-Goals reside in your performance, you need to do a self-assessment to see where you are and where you want to go.)

- What is most important in your life?
- What's working in your life?
- What's not working in your life?
- What is working with your time management?
- How is your time management not working?
- In which areas do you procrastinate?
- What finally breaks the procrastination?
- How can you create closeness with people who are important to you?
- To feel good about your life, what has to happen?
- To feel good about yourself, what has to happen?
- If talking to the Genie from *Aladdin*, what would you wish for? And what if you could have anything you wanted (even if in real time it required five years), what would you wish for? (You must vocalize this. You cannot hit a vague target.)

To complete their Effort-Goals, I coach my clients to use a *Self-Leadership Chart*. On the chart, the vital daily tasks are noted and a grid of Monday through Sunday is used.

Checking the Chart every day helps my clients keep their vital tasks in mind.

Achieve Your Marketing Goals by Using a Phone Script

A major Effort-Goal is: Prepare and rehearse for phone calls that are your first contact with a prospective client.

Your Phone Call Written Script

It is crucial to use a written script. You gain clarity as you write it. You also have something to rehearse with so that you are concise when talking with a new contact on the phone. (You can modify some of your language so that you sound spontaneous during a phone call. However, having a Phone Call Written Script gives you a solid outline to work from.)

Elements of the Phone Call Written Script:

The objective
The opening
Lists of questions
If-Then alternatives for your presentation
Positive closes

The Objective

Here is an example:

Get a commitment for a 15-minute in-person meeting with the prospect.

The Opening

Here is an example:

"Hello, Sam. I'm Susan Johnson, vice-president of new business, for XY Company. We help people improve their productivity by 73%. Is this a good time to talk?"

List of Questions

You need questions to discover what is most important to your prospective client. The person's answers will guide you for what you say next. The prospect's responses give you a view of the jigsaw puzzle pieces that you put into your presentation. For example, you ask, "Have you brought outside trainers into your department before?...And how did it go for you?" You then know what the prospect likes or dislikes about standard training. You're at the beginning of having a roadmap for what points to cover.

If-Then Alternatives for Your Presentation

Here are some examples:

1) If the prospect says, "No, we haven't hired outside training before," then you can respond, "Oh, how do you make sure that your team members can use new software productively?"

2) If the prospect says, "Yes, we've hired trainers before, but I didn't see how it really helped," then you can say, "Oh, tell me more about that…"

By rehearsing If-Then scenarios, you will be able to respond to any answer your prospect gives.

Positive Closes

Always end the phone call on a positive note, no matter how the prospect has responded.

Here are examples:

Prospect says 'yes': "Thanks so much for setting the appointment with me. I'll see you on Thursday at 2 pm. Have a great afternoon."

Prospect says 'no': "Well, thanks for your time and considering this XY product. Oh, who do you know who would be interested in the benefits we talked about?"

Prospect says 'no, I don't know anyone who would like it': "Well, thanks anyway. Perhaps, at some time XYC company may have a match for your firm's future needs. A great day to you."

(form)
Your Phone Call Written Script (sample – filled in)

a) The Objective (Remember: Every business relationship you start can create $10,000 or more for your firm over time.)
Set appointments for 15-minute, in-person meetings.

b) The Opening
"Hello Sam. I'm Tamara Johnson, vice-president of new business for XY Company. We help people improve their productivity by 73%. Is this a good time to talk?"

c) List of Questions
1) Have you brought trainers into your department before? And how did it go for you?

2) Where would you like to be ideally, and what obstacles are between you and there?

3) What software has slowed down your team members—in terms of the learning curve?

4) What do you need from me so that you're ready to move forward on this?

5) What is the usual process for making a decision like this in your department?

d) If-Then Alternatives for Your Presentation
1) IF the prospect says, "No, we haven't hired outside training before."

THEN, I respond, "Oh how do you make sure that team members can use new software productively?"

2) IF the prospect says, "Yes, we've hired trainers before,

but I didn't see how it really helped."

THEN I respond, "Oh, tell me more about that . . ."

3) IF the prospect says, "We've already spent our budget for training this quarter."

THEN I respond, "That's okay. We book out months ahead. Let's talk about your future needs."

4) IF the prospect says, "Our budget is overloaded."

THEN I respond, "Oh, has there been a time when there was something the department really needed, and your team did something creative about the budget? . . . How did that go?"

5) IF the prospect says, "I don't have time right now to talk with you."

THEN, I respond, "What would be a better time? This afternoon? 2pm or 4pm?"

e) Positive Closes

1) "Oh, thanks for your time. So I'll email you the___, and you're going to talk with [person]. Then, I'll call back [time and date]. Is it realistic that you'll be able to connect with [person] before then?"

2) "Oh, thanks for your time. Who do you know who would benefit from the advantages we just talked about? Perhaps, someone you met at a trade association—or in another department?"

***** **End of Above Form** *****

In summary, it helps your morale to have separate Effort-Goals and Result-Goals. Effort-Goals you control, such as how much rehearsal you do with your Phone Call Written Script before you make your marketing phone calls for the day. A Result-Goal can be something like: Gain 8 in-person appointments per week.

Log the results of your work with Effort-Goals. Reward yourself for your efforts.

Also, keep track of the Result-Goals you attain. If you're disappointed with the rate of accomplishing your Result-Goals, change your methods. Hone your techniques.

Points to Remember:

Principle: Honor Effort-Goals and Results-Goals

Power Questions:
What are your Effort-Goals [efforts that you can make]? What are your Result-Goals? Where can you get more training so that you can refine your efforts?

* * * * * *

Because selling (and changing the world) is a demanding profession, I'm including an *encouraging* and empowering article here from author Mark Sanborn:

10 Ideas You Need if You Want to Succeed
by Mark Sanborn

1. Do what you need to do now so you will eventually get to do what you want to do later.

2. Discipline is the ability to get things done regardless of how you feel about doing them.

3. Passion only pays off when channeled into productive effort.

4. Others may believe in you, help you and support you but ultimately nobody will do it for you. You are responsible for your own life.

5. If you don't do your job any differently than anybody else who does it, you won't get paid more than anybody else.

6. More often than not, you succeed in spite of not because of your circumstances.

7. If you think a little better and work a little harder you will always accomplish more than others.

8. If you can't control it, get over it.

9. If you don't appreciate where you are at, you won't appreciate where you are going.

10. Get clear on what really matters to you and then get busy pursuing it.

If you want more insights into how to turn the ordinary into the extraordinary, see Mark's book *Fred 2.0: New Ideas on How to Keep Delivering Extraordinary Results*.

* * *

3 Ways to Renew Your Resolve

Three of the saddest words I know are "I used to..."

I frequently encounter people who tell me they used to

practice the Fred philosophy. They used to be of service in the community. They were once committed to excellent service. But not anymore.

What happened?

The common explanation is they lost their passion and enthusiasm. They got tired, burned out, or discouraged. The challenges of life overcame their commitment, and they lost heart.

If you truly desire to be extraordinary, you have to keep your commitment vital and ongoing. It may be time to renew your resolve.

Here are a few ways to help get you started...

1. Decide to be happy here and now.
According to speaker and author Charlie "Tremendous" Jones, "If you can't be happy where you are, it's a cinch you can't be happy where you ain't." I've never met an unhappy Fred (If you're unfamiliar with my work, a "Fred" is a term I use to describe someone who doesn't settle for normal. Who, like my mailman Fred, chooses to be extraordinary.) I'm sure Freds have times when they're unhappy—we all do—but I've never met a consistently sour Fred. That demeanor just doesn't go with the spirit of Fred. The truth is, if you're not basically happy, you'll have a hard time spreading happiness to others. You can't give what you don't have. Science backs up what Freds inherently know—Freds not only live better; they also live longer. A thirty-year study by Mayo Clinic found that optimists live longer than pessimists. It turns out that looking on the bright side and letting go of

things you can't control is good for your health! We all have our lot in life (and sometimes it feels like a used car lot to me!). Life isn't easy. But often it's simpler than we make it. We have a choice: we can change our lot or we can accept it. If we aren't able to change our lot in life, despite our best efforts, we're down to one option: accept it. But the way we accept it makes all the difference. We can expend our energy kicking and screaming against the injustice of our situation, or we can accept with grace and magnanimity the conditions we can't control. Freds, I've come to believe, go one step beyond. They don't just change their lot in life; they help others live on a better lot too.

2. Try something different.

Are you employed where you really want to work? If not, what steps are you taking to find more meaningful and rewarding work? While it's wise to find a career that's a good fit for you, don't make the mistake of thinking a different environment is necessarily going to solve all your problems. People often think they will be happy if they could just find a different job. However, I've observed that unhappiness tends to follow people. If you aren't happy now, a different job probably won't make you happy either. A better alternative might be to do your current job differently. Have you ever seen a police officer wearing earphones while directing traffic and having his or her own private dance session, waving arms and tooting a whistle? It's enjoyable for motorists to observe, but more than that, I have to believe it makes directing traffic a lot more fun for the police officer too. An ordinary employee might think that the job of directing traffic is drudgery. But a Fred thinks, I'm doing the work I've been given to do here, so why not make the most of it? I shared this story when I was speaking recently, and an audience member approached me afterward. "I directed a lot of traffic in the aftermath of Hurricane Katrina," he said. "It was really stressful. People were angry and on edge. But a funny thing happened. When we started having fun directing traffic—being more patient and engaging motorists in a positive way—they responded in kind. They offered us food, told us jokes, and conversed with us. It made the situation better all the way around." Helen Keller said that life is either a daring adventure or nothing. There is satisfaction in knowing that you do extraordinary work simply by choice. It is also gratifying to be extraordinary for the sake of others who are facing trials. You have the opportunity to make their journeys a little more enjoyable, and along the way you'll find that your journey improves as well. You can suffer through your work, or you can surf through the day, adding as much happiness and fun as you possibly can. Nobody can make that choice but you.

3. Remind yourself regularly.

Remembering to make doctor's appointments, pick up milk on the way home, return those DVDs, and get your oil changed takes up lots of memory. By now you have probably developed different ways to remember those important things you're supposed to do. Sometimes when we're making life changes, our biggest challenge is remembering to carry out the decisions we've made. It isn't that we're not committed to taking this step to do something new or implement something better. It just takes a lot less energy to do things the same way we've always done them. The same phenomenon applies to being a Fred. Even if you agree with the Fred philosophy and want to resemble Fred in spirit and behavior, your good intentions will fail if you don't first remember what to do.

This article is a modified excerpt from *FRED 2.0: New Ideas on How to Keep Delivering Extraordinary Results*. Several additional ways to renew your resolve are featured in *FRED 2.0*, now available where books are sold.

Visit www.marksanborn.com/fred2 now to learn how you can gain instant access to a Fred 2.0 "EXTRAordinary Results" Resource Kit.

Mark Sanborn is the president of Sanborn & Associates, Inc., an idea lab for leadership development. Leadershipgurus.net lists him as one of the top 30 leadership experts in the world. Mark has authored 9 books and more than two dozen videos and audio training programs. He has presented over 2200 speeches and seminars in every state and 12 foreign countries. His book, *The Fred Factor: How Passion in Your Work and Life Can Turn the Ordinary into the Extraordinary* has sold over 1.1 million copies. His latest books are *FRED 2.0: New Ideas on How to Keep Delivering Extraordinary Results; Up, Down or Sideways: How to Succeed When Times Are Good, Bad, or In Between; You Don't Need a Title to be a Leader: How Anyone, Anywhere Can Make a Positive Difference* and *The Encore Effect: How to Achieve Remarkable Performance in Anything You Do*. Mark is a past president of the National Speakers Association and winner of The Cavett. In 2007 Mark was awarded The Ambassador of Free Enterprise Award by Sales & Marketing Executives International.

MarkSanborn.com

BOOK SIX:
WISDOM FOR TOUGH TIMES AND YOUR POWER TO EXCEL

When you want to change the world and you want to feel better and more fulfilled, you will be stretching and growing. You'll try new things. And there will be trials and disappointments along the way.

To help you strengthen yourself, we will cover these topics:

1. The Secret to Using Your Brain to Energize Your Success
2. How to Feel Most Alive!
3. What to Do About a Money Problem
4. Save Your Money and Time When You Communicate Powerfully

Topic #1:
(Book 6: Wisdom for Tough Times)

The Secret to Use Your Brain to Energize Your Success

What if you could get your brain to turbo-charge your success? Research data informs us of a simple element that we can use in our favor. We'll focus on the G.O. process:

G – go for novelty
O – offer challenges

1. Go for novelty

The brain likes novelty so much that dopamine (a neurotransmitter) is released. Dopamine is released whenever the brain feels that the person has been rewarded. It's important to rotate your interests and hobbies (and work activities) so that you do not become bored.

2. Offer challenges

Your brain likes challenges. Picture how people like to play video games when strategy is called for. Others like to do crossword puzzles and so forth.

If you have a business or are considering a plan to start a business, incorporate a positive challenge. Here is an example. Let's say you want to earn $100,000 in one year with your business. Set up your business to serve:
10 clients at $10,000
100 clients at $1,000 level service
1000 purchases of a $100 product.

Any of the above three goals can yield $100,000 and a number of businesses can benefit from setting up more than one pattern.

The value of novelty and challenge is huge. For example,

I've met a number of people who have lost their way. If you asked, they'd characterize their life as "blah." One person specifically told me, "I wish I could have the energy I had in the 80's. I'm just miserable now."

The insight is: In the 80's, this person had goals and was facing novel challenges.

Be sure to include novelty and challenge into your daily life.

You'll feel exhilarated, on purpose, and more fulfilled.

It's worth it!

* * * * * *

Topic #2
(Book 6: Wisdom for Tough Times)
How to Feel Most Alive!

Looking for more joy and fulfillment? Explore this simple and profound approach to life that can open doors for you. We'll use the N.E.W. process:

N – nurture the questions
E – entertain the new
W – work up to things

1. Nurture the questions

Clients and college students often come to me for techniques and shortcuts to more creativity and greater productivity.

However, there is something other than techniques and answers to foster living in a way that feels exhilarating.

Be patient toward all that is unsolved in your heart and try to love the questions themselves . . . Do not now seek the answers, which cannot be given you because you would not be able to live them. And the point is, to live everything. Live the questions now.
– Rainer Maria Rilke

To live in the questions often relates to taking appropriate risks.

Here are relevant questions:
- How far can you take this?
- What new thing can you attempt?
- What would be a breakthrough for you?
- What support can you get for making a breakthrough?
- What would be new, different, and good about your life when the breakthrough happens?
- How can you make such a breakthrough possible?

In essence, living in the questions means that you leave the door open each day for something great to happen. It means that you do things that can lead to a breakthrough. A writer writes every day not knowing which book or screenplay will be a true success.

How can you do something on a daily basis that builds for a new and positive future?

2. Entertain the new

For something new or a breakthrough to happen, we need to do something novel. When you entertain a guest, you make space for them. You put them at ease. Similarly, you need to make space for new activities.

If you've never painted a picture, perhaps you might give it a try.

Many years ago, Steve Jobs dropped out of college, but

visited a college class on calligraphy. (I shared this story at the beginning of this book and it bears repeating here.) When he addressed a Stanford University audience, Jobs said,

"I decided to take a calligraphy class . . . I learned [about] what makes great typography great. It was beautiful, historical, artistically subtle in a way that science can't capture, and I found it fascinating. [Ten] years later, when we were designing the first Macintosh computer, it all came back to me. And we designed it all into the Mac. It was the first computer with beautiful typography. If I had never dropped in on that single course in college, the Mac would have never had multiple typefaces or proportionally spaced fonts. And since Windows just copied the Mac, it's likely that no personal computer would have them."

Make space for trying something new.

It's not only helpful for career success; it also makes life fun and fascinating.

3. Work up to things

I recently spoke with one of my former college students. He's one of the most talented people I've worked with in the last 13 years. I asked if he was working on something that he could post on YouTube. He is both interested in creating futuristic car and aircraft designs and storytelling. I mentioned that he could say that a futuristic car design was part of his science fiction universe.

One car design may be the start of something that could turn into a series of feature films and graphic novels. This could all begin with a thirty-second YouTube video.

This is an example of working up to bigger things.

Again, you would need to live in the questions. Questions like:

- Could this project be a home run for me?
- Could this design lead to an even better one?
- If I post something on YouTube or my own website, could someone important to my future see it?

Here's an example for starting small and blossoming. Vin Diesel invested in himself by producing, starring, and directing a small, independent film *Strays*. After director Steven Spielberg saw *Strays*, he cast Diesel in his film *Saving Private Ryan*. [For more encouragement to do great things, see my book *Nothing Can Stop You This Year!*]

Show the world what you can do on a small scale.

Open the door.

Live in the question: What possible good could come of this?

* * *

Many of us aim to make big things happen but then go astray. Sometimes are goals are off. Perhaps they're so big that we expect too much too fast. Maybe they're too small and they do not feel exciting or motivating.

That's the reason I'm including the following article by author C.J. Hayden. She writes about new year's resolutions; however, let's look at today as the beginning of a new chapter, a more fulfilling chapter of your life.

New Year; New Commitments for Business Success

by C.J. Hayden

It's the beginning of a new year, and a traditional time for making commitments to change. But according to market researcher Dr. Stephen Kraus, author of *Psychological Foundations of Success*, only 15% of the people who make New Year's resolutions manage to keep them.

One of the reasons our resolutions fail is that we frequently resolve to do things just because we believe we should, instead of choosing goals that are naturally compelling and personally meaningful. Another cause for failure is that we often formulate our resolutions simply as good intentions. Without measurable goals and realistic plans to convert our annual declarations into daily action, they tend to slip away in the face of other responsibilities and conflicting demands on our time.

If one of your resolutions this year was to increase your business success, here are three ways to follow through on that resolve:

1. Commit to make every business decision one that leads to more personal fulfillment.

Every day of the year, you are faced with decisions, some big and some small. Should you pursue a lucrative contract with a client whose project doesn't really appeal to you, or take a chance on going after a smaller piece of business that you find much more exciting? Does it make more sense to attend a networking mixer you know you won't enjoy, but where you might meet several prospective clients, or to have a pleasant, relaxed lunch with one potential referral source?

The reality of an entrepreneur's life is that no one is looking over your shoulder to make you do things you don't like. Tasks that you find too onerous or unpleasant simply won't get done, no matter how many times you put them at the top of your to-do list. You'll find it much easier to follow through on your intentions if your destination is compelling and the journey is enjoyable. Choose to pursue clients you like by using tactics you enjoy, and your success rate will skyrocket.

2. Discover the truth about what you want and what it will take to get it.

In building a business, it's easy to get caught up in all the "shoulds" that you hear and imagine. "You should be going after corporate accounts," the industry veterans say. "You should be making six figures online," the Internet marketing gurus tell you. "Every business should advertise," claim the advertising salespeople. "You should be sticking to familiar territory; don't try anything new," your inner critic cautions.

One of the best things about being self-employed is that you get to set your own agenda—if you have the courage to ignore the "shoulds" and go after what you really want. By all means, listen to informed advice from trusted sources, but then make up your own mind.

If you enjoy working with corporate clients, include them in your target market. If building an online business appeals to you, go for it. If advertising is a proven approach to landing clients in your field, include it in your marketing plan. But if any of the "shoulds" others recommend don't appeal to you, don't make sense for your situation, or just don't feel right, let them go. Map out a path that honors who you truly are, and you'll be more likely to follow it.

3. Make your goals big but your action steps small.

Setting ambitious goals for your business can be thrilling and motivating. A key factor to achieving success is creating a vision grand enough to inspire you beyond your comfort zone. But a bold vision without an achievable action plan to support it can lead to overwhelm, disillusionment, and failure. If you don't believe your goals are possible, you will stop working toward them.

For every resolution you make this year, set a measurable goal. For example, a resolution to earn more could spawn the goal "land two new clients each month." Then decide on a series of steps to take toward each goal. A common mistake is to design action steps that are far too large. "Launch a new website" is not a small step; it's a giant leap.

An action step should be small enough to accomplish in a couple of hours. That way you can continuously see and measure your progress and keep yourself inspired. Some steps need to be taken more than once, like "follow up with prospects." That's okay—just make sure that every time you plan to take a step, you can complete it in less than half a day. If a step will take longer than that, break it down into smaller tasks.

Then be sure to revisit your goals at least monthly and review your action plan weekly. If you want to stay on track with your resolutions, you'll need to keep them in front of you throughout the year.

Making resolutions is easy, but keeping them can be hard. Don't beat yourself up for all the times you made resolutions and didn't keep them. Instead, resolve that this year will be different. Commit to pursuing fulfillment rather than acting from obligation, to following your own agenda, and to taking small steps toward big goals, and this time next year, you'll be rewarding yourself for a job well done.

C.J. Hayden, MCC, CPCC, is the bestselling author of *Get Clients Now!, The One-Person Marketing Plan Workbook, 50 Ways Coaches Can Change the World,* and over 400 articles. C.J. is a business coach and speaker who helps entrepreneurs get clients, get unstuck, and get on purpose. Her company, Wings for Business, specializes in serving independent professionals and solopreneurs.

A popular speaker and workshop leader, C.J. has presented hundreds of programs on marketing and entrepreneurship to corporate clients, professional associations, and small businesses. She has taught marketing for John F. Kennedy University, Mills College, the U.S. Small Business Administration, and SCORE. She contributes regularly to dozens of magazines and websites, including Home Business, RainToday, Salesopedia, and About.com.

Contact C.J. Hayden via www.getclientsnow.com

* * *

We can use goals and tasks to keep us on track for both success and fulfillment. My process is to write down my *Top Six Targets* (for the next day) before I go to sleep each night. I often share with my audiences: "Two for you, two for family, and two for work." These tasks are aligned with my goals so that I experience joy, fulfillment and achievement.

* * * * * *

Topic #3
(Book 6: Wisdom for Tough Times)
What to Do About a Money Problem

Do you face a money problem? Did you know that there are many sources to help you with that? We'll use the N.O.W. process:

N – notice who can offer ideas
O – open to find leverage
W – wonder how to encourage help

1. Notice who can offer ideas
The late author Robert H. Schuller wrote that people do not have a money problem but instead they have an idea problem. Schuller was famous for raising tens of millions of dollars to build sacred buildings.

I invite you to write a list of 10 people who could bring you new ideas for how you can make more money.

For example, author Guy Kawasaki convinced me that for certain self-help and business titles, the hardcover and paperback versions gained more sales than the ebook version. He reported that was the case with his book *Enchantment*, and another author told me of her similar results. I found the idea of turning an ebook into a paperback book to be a good idea. My team immediately converted five of my e-books into paperback books. And yes—people bought the new paperback books. [for free chapters of my books on the topics: persuasion and seduction, negotiation, charisma, film directing, and gaining movie roles—for actors, type in "Tom Marcoux" at Amazon.com]

2. Open to find leverage

Many people who succeed truly do *not* do it alone. Let's say that in your neighborhood, the home owners are all pushing for people to keep their lawns well manicured. What if you have a cash flow problem and you do not have the budget to buy a lawn mower? You could go from house to house to see if a neighbor would loan his or her machine. Or you could encourage the group of neighbors to buy yard maintenance equipment as a group. That's called pooling resources, and it's a source of leverage.

In the 1980's a limited partnership entitled Silver Screen Partners II financed films for The Walt Disney Company to the tune of $193 million. It was reported that dentists and doctors (and others) participated. Some of them probably put money into the limited partnership for "bragging rights." Perhaps some said, "Yes. That's right. I'm one of the investors behind *The Little Mermaid*."

My point is that companies do this process all the time; they gather people together to get something done.

You can do the same. More about that in the next step . . .

3. Wonder how to encourage help

Currently, I'm reading a book by Kristine Carlson (co-author with her late husband Richard Carlson of *Don't Sweat the Small Stuff in Love*). In her book *Heartbroken Open*, she writes of one New Year's weekend during a heavy rain which caused a catastrophic mudslide, blocking a road. She and her husband were worried about elderly neighbors being prevented from receiving medical assistance if emergency trucks could not get through.

Richard and Kristine pitched in and moved a lot of mud! However, Richard severely strained his back in the process. Kristine later lamented that they had not called their athletic friends to help. Why? They did not want to disturb their friends' holiday weekend.

Please note this: **It is okay to ask for help**. In fact, when you ask, you sometimes share an adventure with the person/people who help you get something done. Imagine how the friends would tell tales: "Yeah, remember the mudslide of 20xx? What an experience that was! What a good workout. And champagne at Joe's house was a blast."

How do you get people to help you? Three words: Help them first. In fact, I call these the three magic words of networking: Help them first.

Also, when you ask someone if they might help you, remember these elements:

a) Mention the benefits the person will get

b) Make it simple and easy to help you

* * *

Do you need to make more money?

Find a way to gather friends. For example, a friend could film a video that you can use for a Kickstarter.com campaign. A different friend could help you brainstorm what "gifts" you can offer for different levels of contributions to your project.

Start with looking for a way to serve other people with your talents and skills.

The more you are motivated by love, the more fearless and free your action will be. – The Dalai Lama

Many of us need to connect with the idea that working and earning money is one way we participate in doing good in this world.

Work is love made visible. – Khalil Gibran

Keep a notepad or audio recorder near your bed. It's likely that good ideas may arrive in the middle of the night or upon your awakening in the morning.

Many years ago, Jack Canfield said a prayer for receiving a best-selling title for some books. He woke up at 3:30 AM and wrote down 22 titles. One title, with the substitution of "soul" for the word "spirit," led to the *Chicken Soup for the Soul* series of books (200 titles).

The original book has sold over 100 million copies in 54 languages worldwide.

That is the power of a good idea.

Make space for good ideas to come to you. And take action.

Speaking of good ideas, they'll come to you as you stay engaged with what others are doing. For example, I was glancing at a friend's website and I found a video that she did that I feel illustrates how to work to improve one's money situation. Here's a lightly edited transcript of Morgana Rae's video:

5 Secrets to Add 1,000 Ezine Subscribers a Month
by Morgana Rae
(a lightly edited transcript of her video)

I'm going to share my [e-subscribers] list building secrets. I was asked to share how I grew my list to 16,000 so quickly. I want to give my list building strategies so you can do it, too. So I have five; we're going to start with number one.

Secret #1: Have a Really Big, Obnoxious Opt-in Box On Your Website

I believe the number one job of any web page is to get your visitor to take action. And the most important action of any web site is to get them to give you their information so that you can continue to communicate with them and serve them and build a relationship. So create an irresistible offer. And then make it crystal clear that the most important thing that you want them to do on their first visit to your website is to give you their name and their email address.

Secret #2: "Be Santa Claus"

Do as many free interviews and free articles and give as much free advice as you can. Be generous and always include your website address so that when they go to your website, they see your big, ridiculously in-their-face Opt-in offer. And they give you their name and email address. Have an Opt-in box whenever you do a tele-class interview or a radio interview, give away a free handout or a free gift. I added more than a thousand people from a one-hour tele-class (Thank you, Vrinda Norman) that I did in April because I offered a free gift and an Opt-in. So whether people bought or not, I still grew my list and they'll buy later or at least they'll get value.

Secret #3: Be Generous with Testimonials

If there is a person, product or service that you love, share it with the world. Tell everybody. Write a blurb. Shoot a video and when you say your name include your website address. And then people who are curious will go and take a look at your website. And if you gave a good testimonial, the person [you recommended] will be sharing your words, your video everywhere. So you get all these backlinks to your website and Google loves you. And it's just a karmic love fest.

Secret #4: Email Your Subscribers All the Time

I know it's counterintuitive because you'll get unsubscribes every time you send out an email, but the people who stay are going to love you. They're going to feel more connected and more in relationship with you the more often you email out. So send out an email at least every week. I was so polite for so many years; I started my e-zine at the end of 2002. I would send out one little email once a month forever. And I was not growing my list until I started sending out emails at least one or two a week. Even though I get unsubscribes, my list grows faster and faster the more I email out.

Secret #5: Always Have a Mechanism for Getting a List of Your Customers If You're Doing a Joint Venture and Your Partner is Processing the Sales

Always make sure that you have a way to get the names and email addresses of the people who already love you and bought your stuff. Yesterday, I added 400 people to my list who already bought my stuff. Those are my favorite people to add.

Bonus Secret #6: Shoot Videos

Shoot videos like this [the video that is the source of this article]. I mean low tech. This is my iPhone on a tripod. Shoot videos because Google owns YouTube so Google is going to put your videos at the top of the search engine if they like your keywords and people like your video. So the more you do it, the more relaxed you're going to be. Just be a human being. And shoot videos, post them on YouTube, post the YouTube video onto your blog, and then tell the world (Facebook, LinkedIn, Twitter, etc.). And of course always [refer to] your e-zine (enewsletter).

I hope this was helpful to you. Namaste.

MORGANA RAE is the international #1 best selling author of *Financial Alchemy: Twelve Months of Magic and Manifestation*. A sought after teacher, speaker and pioneer in personal development, she is widely regarded to be the world's leading Relationship with Money coach. Morgana's groundbreaking program for creating wealth has featured her on ABC-TV, PBS, NPR, CNN, FOX News Radio, United Press International and The Wall Street Journal online. She wrote the "Life Magic" column for a national women's magazine, and was named a Top Woman In E-commerce by *WE Magazine* in 2012. Morgana's been a featured expert alongside Deepak Chopra, Marianne Williamson, Christopher Howard, Bob Doyle, and T Harv Eker. Morgana's books, CDs, magazine articles, and classes have impacted the lives of hundreds of thousands of people worldwide. Morgana writes, speaks, and coaches from a desire to empower idealistic entrepreneurs, coaches, authors and artists to have a big impact in the world... and to heal the rift between heart, spirit, and money.

www.MorganaRae.com
wecare@morganarae.com

* * *

To continue with strategies to increase income, I'm now including this following article by Lois Creamer.

Talking Money!
by Lois Creamer

One of the most challenging things that speakers do is to talk about themselves and money. I hear it all of the time. When I do programs at chapters I am asked about this more than anything else.

One of the things I say is this: talk about yourself and money as if you are talking about a commodity. Think of your intellectual properties as your product (because it is!) Perhaps that will make it easier if you have that as your thought. You're talking about your "product".

Money is a qualifier to me. If your prospect doesn't bring it up, you need to. Don't ignore this part of the conversation only to waste time and energy only to find out you are way out of their budget. It's a mistake many early in their careers make often.

When talking about your fee, say it confidently, joyfully and expectantly! "My fee is $10,000 plus travel expenses. Is that a fit?" Then shut up! Wait to hear a yes, no, or a maybe. Following is what to do in any case.

If they say "yes", you're in! That's if your open on that date and they are interested in your topic. It's a beautiful thing!

If they say "maybe" they mean that they are unsure of their budget at this time. It's neither yes, nor no. It means you need to ask "When will you know if I am a fit?" And, follow up with them then.

If they say "no" you need to ask "How far apart are we?" This is where the conversation can get interesting! If you are far apart, there are a number of tactics you can take. You may say, "I can't accept that as my fee. I have agents and bureaus all over the country marketing me at my fee and it would be unethical and unfair for me to undercut their efforts on my behalf." ARGUE WITH THAT! What are they going to say? Damn you for being ethical? This is the tact bureaus want you to take.

If you are quoted a low fee you may also take the opportunity to refer another. You may say, "Would you like me to see if I can find someone *less experienced* who may be available?"

If you are close enough that you want to pursue the job, say "If I could do that, what else of value might you be able to offer?" Then, listen to what the prospect has to say. If they ask you what value you would like check out my post "How Do You Define Value?"

at http://bookmorebusiness.com/blog/how-do-you-define-value/

So, if your idea of compensation is an exact match, try one of my tactics and see if it makes a difference. You never know unless you try! Good luck!

—

Copyright 2012 Lois Creamer. Lois works with professional speakers who want to book more business, make more money and avoid costly mistakes! She can be reached in the following ways:

Lois@BookMoreBusiness.com
Phone: 314.822.8225
Twitter: @loiscreamer
Facebook: http://www.facebook.com/loiscreamer
LinkedIn: http://www.linkedin.com/loiscreamer
For more information on Lois' business check out http://www.bookmorebusiness.com as well as http://www.bookmorebusiness.tv!
Sign up so you don't miss a blog post at

http://www.BookMoreBusiness.com/blog

* * *

As I've emphasized multiple times in this book, rehearsal is crucial. At one point, I rehearsed with friends so that when I discussed my fees with a prospective client, I had *no* hesitation. It's vital to be come across as confident in the value that you bring to the client. Of course, you're worth the fee that you're asking. Your confidence becomes their confidence in you.

* * * * * *

Topic #4
(Book 6: Wisdom for Tough Times)
Save Your Money and Time When You Communicate Powerfully

Have you heard that a lot of stress is avoidable? How? Communicate with precision. We'll use the W.O.W. process:

W – write notes
O – offer to repeat their words
W – work out a form

1. Write notes
Taking notes during interactions has literally saved me thousands of dollars. I note the time, date, and person I'm talking with. I send a follow-up email with my notes included. I know of a person who gained $100,000 when he said to someone on the other side of the table: "Okay. Let's

look at my notes and your notes." The other side failed to have thorough notes.

Taking notes and writing them into a follow-up email message creates a "paper trail." Assumptions lead to slipped deadlines and big misunderstandings that suck up time like the undertow at the beach. Protect yourself: take excellent notes and file them.

2. Offer to repeat their words

How do you know that you've truly understood someone's intent? Repeat much of their words back to them. It can sound like: "So I heard you to say Part One of Project 1-2-3 is most important. Do I have that about right?"

At that point, the other person will add to or correct your interpretation. (For more about communicating powerfully, see my book *Be Heard and Be Trusted*.)

3. Work out a form

At one point, I heard someone talk about how her client returned with anger about expectations that were not met.

In response to her question, I suggested: "How about having a form to fill out at the beginning of a project?"

I further invited the business owner to think through how such a form would include a series of questions to pinpoint the client's expectations and the scope of the project. The purpose of this form is to ensure that the client's expectations are realistic and can be fulfilled. It helps to provide a "scorecard" so that the business owner will create a delighted client who is eager to provide a testimonial and referrals for new business.

Here's an example of a few questions that one writer can use as a survey form before adapting a book into a screenplay for a new client:

a) What's the main theme of your book?

b) What is a scene that must be in the screenplay?

c) Summarize the point or theme of your book in one sentence:

(an example of a summarized theme from the film Tootsie: "A man becomes a better man by portraying a woman.")

* * *

As you can see from the above questions, using a form can help both client and contractor identify vital elements of a project.

Using the W.O.W. process saves you time and money.

Avoid needless frustration.

Then you have more energy and less stress.

You'll be more able to apply yourself to productive and profitable pursuits.

A FINAL WORD AND THE SPRINGBOARD TO YOUR DREAMS

Congratulations on your efforts with this book. Realize you can truly change the world. Imagine that you're connected with all that is good in the universe. Now, some of us might say, "I'm looking for love."
Imagine a shift to "I *am* love."

Love is the real work of your life. — Robert Holden

The decision to be the presence of love is the most powerful influence you can have in any situation in your life and in this world. — Robert Holden

Imagine that whatever you're doing it is a possibility to express love and kindness.

How many times have you gone into a store and a clerk was kind and helpful? Didn't that brighten your day?

For me, it was a big shift when I connected to the idea of love being the overarching umbrella. I've held many jobs:

selling cookware, selling pants, acting as a short order cook, or administrative assistant to a bank vice-president and his team of four managers (a nearly impossible job).

In each job, I found ways to be helpful and pleasant.

Work is love made visible. – Khalil Gibran

I now enjoy various other opportunities (author, graduate school instructor, speaker, feature film producer, graphic novel creator/team leader) and I'm convinced that my helpful efforts attracted new possibilities. I have, for years, consistently demonstrated kindness, trustworthiness and competence.

Now it's your turn. Where can you turn up the power on your demonstrating kindness, trustworthiness and competence?

As we come to the close of this book, I'm grateful to have had the opportunity to share insights with you.

To gain more value from this book, be sure to go through it and develop your own To Do List. Take some action. Any action towards improving skills and promoting yourself is helpful. I often say, "Better than zero."

Please consider gaining special training through my coaching (phone and in-person), workshops and presentations.

As you continue to work to change the world you are likely to come up against some tough situations. To be supportive I've written nine books in the following series. . .

- Darkest Secrets of Charisma,
- Darkest Secrets of Persuasion and Seduction Masters: How to Protect Yourself and Turn the Power to Good
- Darkest Secrets of Negotiation Masters

- Darkest Secrets of Making a Pitch to the Film and Television Industry
- Darkest Secrets of Film Directing
- Darkest Secrets of the Film and Television Industry Every Actor Should Know
- Darkest Secrets of Business Communication: Using Your Personal Brand
- Darkest Secrets of Spiritual Seduction Masters
- Darkest Secrets of Small Business Marketing

See my blog at
www.BeHeardandBeTrusted.com

The best to you and may you continue to change the world,
Tom
Tom Marcoux,
America's Communication Coach
Motion Picture Director, Actor, Producer, Screenwriter
P.S. See **Free Chapters** of Tom Marcoux's 20 books at http://amzn.to/ZiCTRj

Titles include:
Be Heard and Be Trusted
Nothing Can Stop You This Year
Truth No One Will Tell You
10 Seconds to Wealth
Your Secret Charisma
Wake Up Your Spirit to Prosperity
The Cat Advantage
— and more.
(For coaching, reach Tom Marcoux
at tomsupercoach@gmail.com)

EXCERPT FROM
BE HEARD AND BE TRUSTED: HOW YOU CAN USE SECRETS OF THE GREATEST COMMUNICATORS TO GET WHAT YOU WANT

2nd Edition by Tom Marcoux, America's Communication Coach

Table of Contents

How You Can Radiate Charisma
* Guest Article by Dr. Tony Alessandra
How Billionaires & Millionaires Use C. O. M. P. E. L.
Handle Fear & Mistakes with Skill
* Guest Article by Dr. Fred Luskin
Reduce Risk
* Guest Article by Dr. Elayne Savage
Power Thought / Physiology Process
Solution-for-Error Plan
How to Help People Feel at Ease

Overcome the #1 Obstacle to Happiness
Truth No One Will Tell You
Great Communicators Win with Job Interviews
* Guest Article by Mike Robbins
Win When Dealmaking and Negotiating
Be Heard and Be Trusted on the Telephone
How to Use Your Personal Brand as Your Shortcut to Trust
Great Communicators Make Good Luck
* Guest Article by Marc Allen
* Guest Article by Linda and Charlie Bloom
Great Communicators Give Compelling Speeches
* Guest Article by Jay Conrad Levinson
Great Communicators Persuade with Ease
Secrets about Networking and the Media
* Guest Article by Guy Kawasaki
A Final Word and Springboard to Your Dreams
Special Offer for Readers of this book .
Excerpt from Darkest Secrets of Persuasion and Seduction Masters
by Tom Marcoux
About the Author

* * * * * *

Part I, Section 1
How You Can Radiate Charisma
and Get What You Want

What terrific things could be in your life if you were charismatic?

Imagine if you could easily gain people's agreement and

cooperation. Top professionals come across as charismatic. *The American Heritage Dictionary* defines "charisma" as "personal magnetism or charm."

A charismatic person makes each of us feel like the most important person in the room. How is this done? The charismatic person listens to others and connects with their pain.

A charismatic person often uses an effective story to engage people's emotions and open listeners to benevolent influence.

A charismatic person expresses compelling messages. Dictionary.com defines "compelling" as "to force or drive, especially to a course of action … to overpower … to have a powerful and irresistible effect, influence." We want to overpower inertia, low moods, and procrastination. We want to take action consistently to create the best possible situations in our own lives.

An interviewer said to me, "I'm not comfortable with the idea of 'force.'"

"All right, let's focus on having a good intention first," I replied. "Instead of force, let's aim to 'move' a person's emotions. "For example, when I was ten years old, my piano teacher knew how to persuade me to practice. She helped me see how much I improved when I practiced. She moved my emotions so that I could feel and enjoy the benefits I was getting. She also cleverly had me practice a song that I really wanted to play."

In essence, my piano teacher was a compelling communicator. She was heard and trusted by me. And that's what you'll learn how to do in this book.

How much would your life improve if you could easily get people to say yes to you? What if you could easily get them to want to say yes?

- "Yes! You're hired. The job is yours."
- "Yes! Here's your raise and promotion."
- "Yes! I'll marry you."
- "Yes! Here's $200,000 to develop your entrepreneurial idea."
- "Yes! I'll buy your product."

What if you could get what you really want – faster than you ever imagined?

That was both the opportunity and the problem for my client Sarah. She confessed, "I need to improve my communication skills."

"How would that give you what you really want?" I asked.

For a moment, she frowned in thought.

"And what do you really want?"

"A raise and a promotion!" she said with sudden clarity.

"What would that take?"

"My boss would have to trust me with higher profile assignments."

In essence, Sarah didn't just want to improve her communication skills; she wanted to be heard and be trusted.

With my guidance, Sarah learned to use the skills found in this book. She learned methods to increase her confidence, speak well to authority, and feel higher self-esteem.

For 26 years, I have helped thousands of clients and audience members become great communicators. In fact, an earlier version of this book was accepted as a textbook by Cogswell Polytechnical College and included in that college's time capsule.

The capsule is set to be opened in 2100. Even in 2100, the timeless principles of warm and trustworthy communication will be valuable.

In this book, we will cover story after story that highlight how many, including twelve billionaires and millionaires, communicate successfully to make things happen. You will also learn directly from the articles and comments of a number of other great communicators.

This book is filled with principles that can help you relate to people on a higher level of connection and cooperation.

As to methods there may be a million and then some, but principles are few. The man who grasps principles can successfully select his own methods. The man who tries methods, ignoring principles, is sure to have trouble. - Ralph Waldo Emerson

For compelling communication, you need to do two things:

1. Seize the attention
2. Create a connection

We want our communication to be not merely pleasant, but compelling. We want people to cooperate with us, to take action in the direction we're proposing. To help you make this year the best year of your life so far, we will explore the C.O.M.P.E.L. process.

C - Connect with the listener's pain
O - Open with genuineness
M - Maximize leverage
P - Pull with a story

E - Ease
L - Lift

"Be so good – they can't ignore you," said writer-actor-comedian Steve Martin in response to the question, "How do you gain big success?" With this book, you will become so good at influencing people. And, I will add, be so trustworthy that they want to do for you.

Let's move on. Let's learn how to be charismatic and influential …

Connect with the Listener's Pain

Where does it hurt? Did your attention go to your body? Did you feel tension in your neck area?

To make your message compelling, you need to uncover your listener's pain.

Ask someone what he or she wants. The easiest way for the person to reply is to say, "What I don't want is to stay in this job.

Here's what I do not like in my current situation." The person talks about what causes pain.

What I have in my heart must come out; that is the reason I compose. - Ludwig van Beethoven

Beethoven reminds us that what is in our hearts must come out. Similarly, as great communicators we need to help our listener express his or her heartfelt pains and desires. By helping your listener identify "where it hurts," you can help her achieve a transformation.

The power of transformation reminds me of the journey of Gay Hendricks, the bestselling author of *Five Wishes* and cofounder of The Hendricks Institute. Years ago, when he was a 300-pound tobacco addict in a horrible marriage, he felt the need to reinvent himself. He says that what sustained him was a deep inner knowledge of where he was going – toward a life of soul awareness and creative fulfillment. Today he has a fit,

180-pound frame, over six feet tall. Gay was blocked. His blockage was made of conflicted feelings: he couldn't decide whether to continue studying in the University of New Hampshire counseling program or follow his desire to be a writer. Dwight Webb, an insightful professor of his, suggested, "Why not write about counseling?" Was there any reason Gay could not put his feelings and inner experiences into poems and articles connected with his profession? The answer was that he could do both things he loved. He could pursue psychological counseling and writing. Gay's poems were published in counseling journals and caught the eye of a professor at Stanford University, who helped Gay gain a fellowship to that institution for his doctorate. Gay went on to a 25-year academic career and wrote over 20 books.

When I contacted Gay a while ago, I discovered that he had found fulfillment as a screenwriter-filmmaker and as a seminar leader through The Hendricks Institute. Gay's journey shows that it is an "and" universe, not a "this or that" universe. The point is that Gay's professor Dwight Webb provided great coaching. He listened to Gay's pain and shared a new way to view the situation.

The only service a friend can really render is to keep up your courage by holding up to you a mirror in which you can see a noble image of yourself. - George Bernard Shaw

When you really want to be heard and be trusted, focus

on something that will benefit the other person. Be the person's friend. Take the appropriate actions to help him or her.

With a number of my clients, we focus on the transition from novice salesperson to coach-to-action. As George Bernard Shaw points out, you as the coach can hold a friendly mirror up to your listener, who will then be able to see a noble image of the self. This noble image can inspire the listener to agree to whatever you're offering. And as the coach, you can help the person enjoy more in life and work.

It is above all by the imagination that we achieve perception and compassion and hope. - Ursula LeGuin

First, connect with the listener's pain. Then, with the knowledge you have gained, you can focus on helping. You can help people imagine a better personal future.

People in general are starved for the experience of being heard. - Gordon Livingston, M.D.

Get what you want by giving people what they crave: to be heard.

Principle:
Connect with the listener's pain and show that you have the remedy.

Power Question:
How can you gently ask questions that allow you to identify the listener's pain?*

*NOTE: * To get the maximum benefit from this book, devote at least 20 seconds to writing down the answer to each Power Question in your personal journal.*

Open with Genuineness

When you are content to be simply yourself and don't compare or compete, everybody will respect you. - Lao-tzu

"We don't need you to be perfect; we need you to be genuine," I say to my graduate students who seek to be better public speakers and pitch-givers.

Do what you said you were going to do,
when you said you were going to do it,
in exactly the way you said you were going to do it.
You won't ever get any better business advice than that.
Be there when you said you would be there.
Deliver when you said you would deliver.
Call when you said you would call.
Be a person who can be counted on
by keeping his word every time.
- Larry Winget

Have you ever been afraid that when you are giving a speech, your mind might go blank or you might lose your place? The solution is, *be genuine.*

When I coach CEOs and company presidents in how to give speeches, I help them express genuineness. This helps the CEO connect with the audience and motivate team members.

End of Excerpt from
Be Heard and Be Trusted: How You Can Use Secrets of the Greatest Communicators to Get What You Want
Copyright 2012 Tom Marcoux Media, LLC

Purchase your copy of this book (paperback or ebook) at Amazon.com or BarnesandNoble.com
See **Free Chapters** of Tom Marcoux's 19 books at http://amzn.to/ZiCTRj

ABOUT THE AUTHOR

Tom Marcoux helps people like you fulfill big dreams. Known as America's Communication Coach, Tom has authored 20 books with sales in 15 countries. One of his *Darkest Secrets* books rose to #1 on Amazon.com Hot New Releases in Business Life (and in Business Communication). He guides clients and audiences (IBM, Sun Microsystems, etc.) to success in job interviewing, public speaking, media relations, and branding. A member of the National Speakers Association, he is a professional coach and guest expert on TV, radio, and print, and was dubbed "the Personal Branding Instructor" by the *San Francisco Examiner*. Tom addressed National Association of Broadcasters' Conference six years running. With a degree in psychology, Tom is a guest lecturer at **Stanford University**, DeAnza, & California State University, and teaches public speaking, science fiction cinema/literature and comparative religion at Academy of Art University. Winner of a special award at the **Emmys**, Tom wrote, directed, and produced a feature film that the distributor took to the **Cannes film market**, and the film gained international distribution. He is engaged in book/film projects *Crystal Pegasus* (children's) and *TimePulse* (science fiction). See TomSuperCoach.com and Tom's well-received blog at www.BeHeardandBeTrusted.com

Tom Marcoux can help you with **speech writing** and **coaching for your best performance.**
As Tom says, *Make Your Speech a Pleasant Beach.*
Join Tom's Linkedin.com group: *Executive Public Speaking and Communication Power.*
Get a **Free** report: "9 Deadly Mistakes to Avoid for Your Next Speech and 9 Surefire Methods" at

http://tomsupercoach.com/freereport9Mistakes4Speech.html

Tom Marcoux has trained CEOs, small business owners, and graduate students to speak with impact and gain audiences' tremendous approval and cooperation. *Learn how to present and get thunderous applause!*

"Tom, Thanks for your coaching and work with me on revising my speech at a major university. Working with you has been so enlightening for me. Through your gentle prodding and guidance I was able to write a speech that connects with the audience. I wish everyone could experience the transformation I have undergone. You have helped me discover the warm and compelling stories that now make my speech reach hearts and uplift minds. This was truly an empowering experience. I cannot thank you enough for your great assistance." — J.S.

Become a fan of Tom's graphic novels/feature films:

Science fiction: *TimePulse*
www.facebook.com/timepulsegraphicnovel

Fantasy Thriller: *Jack AngelSword*
type "JackAngelSword" at Facebook.com

Children's Fantasy: *Crystal Pegasus*
www.facebook.com/crystalpegasusandrose

See **Free Chapters** of Tom Marcoux's 19 books at http://amzn.to/ZiCTRj

Special Offer Just for Readers of this Book:

Contact Tom Marcoux at tomsupercoach@gmail.com for special discounts on books, coaching, workshops and presentations. Just mention your experience with this book.

www.ingramcontent.com/pod-product-compliance
Lightning Source LLC
Chambersburg PA
CBHW060519100426
42743CB00009B/1377